FURTHER SUFFOLK MEMORIES

More stories from Walberswick and Blythburgh people during World War II

SUBSCRIBERS

Atherton, Patricia
Bally, Elsie
Bassett, Eric
Bell, Mervyn and Mary
Bird, John
Block, Edith
Blythburgh Parish Council
CDC Demolition Ltd, Waldringfield
Chapman, Ellen
Clarke, Arthur
Day, Arthur
Day, Jill
Dillon, Brian and Miriam
Dudley, John and Linda
English, George and Doris (New Zealand)
English, Herbert
English, John
Godbold, Margot
Godsmark, Grahame
Harwood, Charles and Margo
Hetherington, Judith
Horsey, R. J.
Hyne, Heather
Josephs, Julia
Kett, Derek
King, Mary
Leighton, Rae
Leverett, John
Locker, Timothy

Moore, David
Morton, Judith and Brian
Mostyn, Richard (Zimbabwe)
Munford, Dennis and Audrey
Osborne, Nan
Pappworth, Jean
Payne, Brian
Rogers, Dulcie
Rowland, Vic
Sexton, Bill
Sharman, Arthur
Sharman, Paul
Sharman, Richard
Shirreff, Dione
Smith, Doris
Smith, Vera
Stanley, Robert
Stannard, Wally and Cissy
Stanyer, John
Stracey, Jeltje
Stringer, Beryl
Thewlis, Joyce (South Africa)
Titford, Irene
Turnbull, Jean
Walberswick Common Lands Charity
Walberswick Parish Council
Walford, Gill
Watson, Les
Wythe, Pat

Further Suffolk Memories

More stories of Walberswick and Blythburgh people during World War II

Compiled by

ARTHUR SHARMAN
and
PATRICIA WYTHE

The Yard Press, Sudbury, Suffolk
2001

Published 2001 by The Yard Press
68 Friars Street, Sudbury, Suffolk, CO10 2AG

ISBN   0 9514910 6 7

© 2001 Arthur Sharman and Patricia Wythe

All rights reserved. No part of this publication may be reproduced, stored in a retrieval system, or transmitted in any form or by any means, electronic, mechanical, photocopying, recording, or otherwise, without the prior permission of the authors.

Cover design from an idea by Richard Sharman, by Radius Design, Sudbury

Printed by Interprint, Malta

Cataloguing-in-Publication Data

A catalogue entry for this publication is obtainable from the British Library

This book is dedicated to the memory of
DAVID SHIRREFF, MC,
a distinguished soldier, colonial administrator and judge, whose inspiration and work in compiling *Suffolk Memories* made it such a great success and who suggested, encouraged, and inspired the compiling of this supplementary volume.

CONTENTS

Subscribers   ii

Foreword by Major General J. B. Dye, CBE, MC, DL   ix

Introduction and Acknowledgements   xi

Contributors and Stories   xiii

A Remembrance Service Tribute   xv

Chapter 1   The Royal Navy   1
A North Atlantic convoy, 1; Life aboard the convoy ships, 19 Antony Cleminson's tailpiece, 22; Another Royal Navy tale, 25; At sea, 30; Medical memories, 35; Combined Operations, 36; Memories of the war 50 years on, 38

Chapter 2   The Army   52
Armoured warfare (1), 52; Armoured warfare (2), 57; The move to New Zealand, 61; A gunner, policeman, and fireman, 66; Memories of home and Far East, 71; Home Guard to National Service gunner, 79; In the Auxiliary Territorial Service (ATS), 84; BEF to Burma, 88

Chapter 3   The Royal Air Force   92
A widow of war, 92; Battle of Britain and onward, 101; One WAAF's wartime experiences, 115

Chapter 4   The Merchant Navy   119
Convoys in home waters, 119

Chapter 5   Flight from Malta   125
A family escapes, 125; Memories of my mother, Lady Mallaby, 139

CONTENTS

Chapter 6   A Reserved Occupation   142
  Building radar stations, 142

Chapter 7   The Nurses   148
  A nurse and soldier's wife, 148; A Naval VAD nurse, 151;
  District and hospital nursing, 155

Chapter 8   Wives and Mothers   158
  A near miss, 158; Home and duty, 166

Chapter 9   Care of Children   170
  Barnardo children, 170; Children from concentration camps, 172

Chapter 10   School Children   176
  Chidhood memories, 176; Three little maids from school, 182

FOREWORD

by Major General J. B. Dye, CBE, MC, DL

This second book of Suffolk Memories, recording stories from Walberswick and Blythburgh, completes the mosaic of reminiscences from people who were associated with these two East Anglian villages during World War II, or subsequently went to live there.

As in the first book, these narratives are extremely diverse and remind us again, not only of acts of individual bravery by combatants, but also highlight the vital role of the people in the villages who, by force of circumstances, had to remain at home. By their fortitude they maintained the morale of the members of their families who were away on active service, frequently through long periods of separation and often without any communication. It was a hard life for them to bear.

These two books provide a fascinating account of the military and social history of the life and times of people from these rural areas, who lived through the dramatic years of the Second Great War of the last century. They are of great interest now, and will provide a source of valuable material for future historians.

Jack Dye
Helmingham, Suffolk
2001

INTRODUCTION AND ACKNOWLEDGEMENTS

Suffolk Memories consisted mainly of stories by the military and of their derring-do, what it was like to be under fire, and the horrors of war. There were stories about the ghastly conditions that prisoners of war had to endure in the Far East and other theatres of war and one story about the unfortunate people who had been imprisoned by the Nazis in the concentration camp at Belsen.

This book, *Further Suffolk Memories*, contains the few stories about the military which the compilers of *Suffolk Memories* were unable to include and which the late David Shirreff was anxious to be recorded. However, it mainly concentrates on the memories of those who for some reason or another had been unable to serve in the Armed Forces. These men and women were in reserved occupations doing essential war work, or wives and mothers keeping the home fires burning, or suffering ill health, or were too old or too young to be directly involved in the conflict.

A number of the contributors of these stories are people who lived in Walberswick and Blythburgh during and before the war but later moved away to another part of the country and in three cases overseas, to Australia, New Zealand, and South Africa.

To give the reader an idea of the context of the time, the compilers have added to some of the stories. Other stories are mostly as the contributor wrote or dictated them, editing being done only to correct the spelling of place names, dates, continuity of events, and other minor details. As the years pass, memories of events tend to become telescoped or out of sequence, and these we have corrected as best we can without detracting from the author's story. However, the compilers take full responsibility for errors.

Over thirty people have contributed their stories mostly through personal interview; others have written their own stories, which the compilers have checked and edited. In some cases, more than one interview was necessary and many telephone calls were made to clear up minor points. We thank the contributors for their patience with us and for their enthusiasm, which has made all our efforts worthwhile.

The compilers wish to thank John Welch for his help, advice, and guidance in many matters, but especially in making sure that our quotations

INTRODUCTION AND ACKNOWLEDGEMENTS

from the book *Convoy* in 'North Atlantic convoy' stayed within Penguin Books' constraints.

We wish to express our grateful thanks to Major General Jack Dye, our local Royal British Legion branch patron, for writing the Foreword, reading and editing the script, correcting our errors, and for his support and encouragement.

Our thanks also go to Brian Dillon for his encouragement, advice, and many helpful suggestions in all the stories; to Alan and Sue Walpole for their help in typing Lady Mallaby's story, 'Flight from Malta'; to Lieutenant Commander G. G. Prall, RN Retired, for his help with the naval stories; and to Richard Sharman for his work on the photographs and maps. We thank Elizabeth Nurser of the Yard Press, Sudbury for her advice and help, and for accepting the commission.

As with *Suffolk Memories* any profits from the sale of this book will, after publication expenses have been met, go to the Walberswick and Blythburgh Branch of the Royal British Legion for its welfare purposes.

Arthur Sharman and Patricia Wythe
Walberswick, May 2001

INDEX OF CONTRIBUTORS AND PERSONS WHOSE STORIES ARE TOLD HERE

Allport, John, 19
Atherton, John ✠, 31
Bally, Elsie, 155
Bird, John, 101
Block, Edith née Glasspool, 158
Chambers, Eileen née Sharman, 195
Clarke, Arthur, 119
Cleminson, Antony, 22
Connick, Richard, 142
Connick, Vida née Flint, 166
Day, Jill née Cady, 182, 183
Dowse, Renée née Kett, 84
English, Doris née Labad, 60, 64
English, Edgar ✠, 1
English, George, 57, 64
English, Herbert
English, Robert ✠, 25
Fairs, Geoffrey ✠, 92
Fairs, Terry, 101
Gilbert, Christine (Tommy) née Cross, 182, 186
Godbold, Margot, 176
Harwood, Charles, 71
Harwood, Margo née Fairs, 148

Kett, Derek, 79
Kett, Donald ✠, 36
Locker, Timothy, 139
Mallaby, Lady Elizabeth formerly Locker née Brooke ✠, 125
Osborne, Nancy née Rogers, 114
Pappworth, Jean, 172
Pymar, Richard, 164
Rogers, Dulcie, 67
Rogers, George ✠, 66
Roxburgh, Ian ✠, 35
Roxburgh, Patricia née Wilson, 151
Sanger, Mary Joy née Sparkes, 170
Smith, David, 31
Smith, Doris formerly Fairs, née Buck, 92
Stanley, Robert, 38
Stanyer, George ✠, 88
Stanyer, John, 88
Stringer, Beryl née Sharman, 182, 193
Thewlis, Joyce née English, 25

✠ Deceased

A REMEMBRANCE SERVICE TRIBUTE

1999 saw the people of Blythburgh and Walberswick, eighty-five years after the start of World War One and sixty years after the outbreak of World War II, pay homage to those who sacrificed their lives in two World Wars in the cause of freedom and justice.

The Chaplain of our Branch of the Royal British Legion, the Reverend Canon John Matthews, conducted the Service of Commemoration. It is thought fitting that his excellent address on these two special anniversaries should be included in this book.

Remembrance Sunday 1999 Walberswick
10.45 am – Parade Service

TEXT: Psalm 37 Verse 3: *'Put thou thy trust in the Lord, and be doing good: dwell in the land, and verily thou shalt be fed.'*

This year is a time for everyone – especially for us as members of the Royal British Legion, deeply rooted as we are in the life of our Nation, to recall many events and the people who have perished and suffered over the years, and must not be forgotten – in the tangled history of this country amidst the complex happenings of the last 100 years.

The development of everyday life has changed beyond recognition and continues to do so at an ever-increasing rate. There are few who remember at first-hand any of the first ten years of this century. We must depend upon reports and perhaps conversations with parents and older relatives who have known the 'Edwardian Era' and life before 1914 when so much in the whole world was altered and swept away by that dreadful conflict which lasted so long till 1918.

As the past 80 years have elapsed we have become accustomed to the accelerating pace of life – faster cars, air travel, T.V. and the whole gamut of electronics and computerisation – all used in both peace and war. These developments and inventions have occurred swiftly in times of peace and even more rapidly in war, when desperate situations called for new techniques. Against the background of such changes we must not overlook the endeavours of those who survived the challenges of war to improve the quality of life and society. As each year we remember the thousands of men, women and children who died or were severely injured in the wars so, too, we should give thanks for the contributions made by those who lived on.

A point has now been reached in the life of all mankind, particularly in the West, when it is more important than ever to take stock of the situation we are in. The ideals set before us by the Royal British Legion are relevant here: care and thought for the past and for those who still need help; vision and understanding for the future.

Many intractable problems face us: moral decline, violence, organised crime, the break up of family life; the need to grapple with the technicalities of the coming age, notably the net with its varied on-line off-shoots such as e-mail and electronic banking and commerce. Again, political questions such as the nature of a Sovereign State stare us in the face and demand our attention.

The future is unknown and unknowable, but the principles which we, as free men and women, should hold to are well known. Goodness, honesty, trust in God. The ethics of God as taught in the Bible should be our guide. Let no one deceive us with clever arguments. St Paul, in many of his letters, had sound advice for his readers, as they sought to serve as Christians in their difficult pagan world of Greece and Rome. For instance to those in Corinth, a notorious centre of wickedness and vice, he wrote: 'Watch ye, stand fast in the faith, quit you like men, be strong'. While to those in Thessalonia he advised: 'Prove all things, hold fast to that which is good'.

And so with us, as we face this New World, with all its possible opportunities for good and all its threats and dangers. We can but honour and remember those who have sacrificed themselves in any way in this tortured 20th century now drawing to a close, by checking everything that comes to our attention, political, sociological, and technological. Those things which we find good we must support and hold fast. Those that we find wrong or false we must jettison and firmly reject.

In many ways we stand at the end of this era as King George VI did in his Christmas Broadcast of 1939 when he said, 'And I said to the man who stood at the gate of the year, "Give me a light that I may tread safely into the unknown" and he replied, "Go out into the darkness and put your hand into the hand of God. That shall be to you better than light and safer than any known way".'

Chapter 1
THE ROYAL NAVY

A North Atlantic Convoy
Edgar Alfred English

The lifeblood of beleaguered Britain was shipping, and all would be lost if the convoys could not get through with their vital supplies. The merchant ships sailing on the North Atlantic run had U-boat wolf packs snapping at their heels and it was the job of the escorting Naval vessels to try to protect them. One of those vessels was HMS *Volunteer* and a member of the crew was Edgar English, who came from a seafaring family living in Walberswick. He was on the North Atlantic convoys from the time he joined *Volunteer* until VE Day.

Edgar, who was the younger brother of Robert and Herbert English (see their stories), was born and bred in Walberswick. He went to the local

Edgar English (back row, left) with his shipmate 'Bunting Tossers' when in HMS Volunteer. *(Photo from Terry Simpson)*

1

HMS Volunteer *in her warpaint. (Photo from Terry Simpson)*

primary school until he was 11 and then completed his childhood education at the Area School in Reydon. Upon leaving school he joined the Royal Navy and served for twenty-two years plus 15 months in boy service. He writes:

> I joined the Royal Navy on 18 June 1941 as a Signal Boy and was sent to HMS *St George* which was a pre-war holiday camp at Douglas, Isle of Man. I signed on to complete 12 years in the Royal Navy and did the full peacetime signal training at HMS *St George*. I left there on 19 November 1942 to join HMS *Volunteer*, an old First World War destroyer of the V class engaged on convoy escort work, mainly in the North Atlantic run, from Liverpool and Newfoundland; she had just come out of dry dock after having a major refit. I was only $18^{1}/_{4}$ and the youngest member of the crew, so was immediately nicknamed 'Nipper'. This name stuck with me until the end of the war.
>
> I remember a convoy leaving with 40 merchant ships and only 27 arriving safely at Liverpool, about a third having been sunk by U-boats. A book simply called *Convoy* was published a few years ago about this particular convoy. We also escorted a couple of convoys to the Azores; these islands belonged to Portugal, which remained neutral during the war, but they loaned them to Britain for the duration.

The convoy Edgar referred to was HX.229. It was involved in a severe battle with the U-boats in the North Atlantic in March 1943. This battle proved to be a turning point in the war against the German submarines;

A NORTH ATLANTIC CONVOY

never again were the U-boats to be so successful in the North Atlantic Ocean. The following story will give the reader some idea of the strain and harsh conditions under which the crews of merchant ships and their naval escorts had to endure. Most of the time the weather was foul, though bad weather could, and sometimes did, prove a blessing to the convoys. Edgar continues:

> HMS *Volunteer* carried three Signalmen and our duties were a four-hour watch on the open bridge followed by eight hours off. When the U-boats attacked though, we all had to go on the bridge for action stations. On the way out whilst escorting a convoy from England the weather had been bitterly cold with rough high seas. Conditions were so bad that one of the Signalmen suffered from continuous seasickness and got frostbite in both feet. He had to go into hospital at St John's but luckily we got a replacement for him or we would have had to do extra watches.

At that particular time HMS *Volunteer* had been escorting the convoy ON.168 from England to St John's and had spent over two weeks battling against severe gales. Her fight against the mountainous seas had caused *Volunteer*'s plates to start and they were leaking so badly that when she arrived at St John's she had to go into dry dock to be repaired. Edgar recalls:

> When the *Volunteer* went into dry dock we went to live in the Canadian Naval Barracks until she would be ready for sea again. It was like heaven to go into a dining room, having three meals a day and to find at breakfast a big churn of lovely cold milk for our cornflakes followed by a beautifully cooked breakfast. The Royal Naval barracks in England didn't even have a dining room or cornflakes. On *Volunteer* it was two meals a day: midday and evening. These were hot meals as long as the seas were not too rough to prevent the pans being kept on the galley ranges. That time, on the way out, we seemed to exist on tins of corned beef or herrings in tomato sauce with hard thick dog-like biscuits.

The time it would take to repair *Volunteer* meant she would not be ready to sail with the Naval escort ships for convoy SC.122, the convoy she had been scheduled to join and which was due to sail from St John's on 11 March. The Canadian Naval authorities at St John's did a reshuffle of escort ships, and *Volunteer* was ordered to sail with convoy HX.229 instead. She would therefore leave St John's on 13 March to meet with that convoy at the

HMS Volunteer *re-oiling in a calm sea. (Photo from Terry Simpson)*

WOMP on 14 March. (WOMP was the acronym for the Western Ocean Meeting Point where convoys rendezvoused to meet up with their convoy escorts).

There was a further complication, however: the Escort Group commander's vessel, of HX.229, HMS *Highlander,* was also in dry dock for repairs and she would not be ready to sail until two days after the convoy was due to leave. Commander E. C. L. Day, RN, the captain of *Highlander* and commander of the Escort Group, rather than transfer to another ship, requested that the convoy be delayed until his vessel was ready to sail. The authorities at St John's were unable to allow this, and HMS *Volunteer took Highlander's* place, with her captain Lieutenant Commander G. L. Luther, RN, appointed Escort Group commander until such time as *Highlander* caught up with the convoy and Commander Day could resume command.

There were 40 merchant ships in HX.229: ten tankers, nine refrigerated ships, and twenty-one freighters of which seven were Liberty ships.

The A*braham Lincoln,* one of the refrigerated ships, was the convoy's Commodore ship under the command of Commodore M. J. D. Mayall, RNR and he was in charge of the merchant ships. No Rescue Ship had been

A NORTH ATLANTIC CONVOY

designated for this convoy, so Commodore Mayall instructed the captains of the merchant ships that, in the event of a ship's being torpedoed, the last ship in the column was to stop and pick up the survivors.

There were six escort ships: four destroyers, HMS *Volunteer, Beverley, Witherington* and *Mansfield,* and *two corvettes, HMS Anemone* and HMS *Pennywort.*

HX.229 with her escorts sailed on the appointed date, 14 March. The following day HMS *Witherington* dropped out, leaving only five escorts. A severe gale was blowing and this worsened during the night. However dawn saw the worst of the storm over but, waiting for the convoy to reach the open ocean and clear the coast of Newfoundland, were some forty U-boats.

The next day, the 15th, saw a severe gale blowing and one can only conjecture how the crew in *Volunteer* was feeling. There would certainly not be much chance of rest or hot food; the only consolation was that, so far, there was no sign of the U-boats.

In the very early hours of the 16th, a U-boat on the surface suddenly realized she was in the middle of the convoy. None of the lookouts on the convoy had spotted the submarine, but fortunately the Admiralty picked up the sighting signal from the U-boat and they advised Lieutenant Commander Luther that the convoy was being shadowed. When notice had

A weary Edgar on his mess deck having a quick snack.
(Photo from Edgar English)

been received of the shadowing, Luther anticipated that it would not be many hours before the U-boats would attack; he decided to have *Volunteer*'s oil tanks topped up: a wise and prudent decision as it turned out.

That evening, Edgar and the crew in *Volunteer* as with those on the other escort ships held intensive practice at action stations in anticipation of a U-boat attack. They didn't have long to wait – Edgar and his shipmates had little chance for rest or food after that.

This is a good point at which to remind the reader what went on in the escort ships when the order 'Action Stations' was given.

> Practice action stations were held on the escorts with more intensity than normal that evening [16 March]. First lieutenants would see that a hot meal was available. The captain of each ship would make his own decision as to when to order full Action Stations; when this did happen, watertight doors would be closed all through the ship, men would have to remain permanently on duty for many hours or possibly days. Each captain left his decision as late as possible but it is probable that by nightfall the crews of many escorts were at Action Stations.
>
> Let the reader spare a thought for Lieutenant-Commander Gordon John Luther. This young professional naval officer had several years of theoretical anti-submarine experience but only one, incident-free, North Atlantic convoy crossing. He must have dreamed many times before then of leading his own destroyer into action against an enemy submarine. As the last of the daylight of 16 March slowly faded, Luther stood on the bridge of *Volunteer* commanding not just one destroyer in action against one U-boat but a weak collection of completely unknown escort vessels – two slow corvettes and two tired old ex-American destroyers in addition to his own ship. The stream of U-boat signals now coming from out of the darkness on the horizon left Luther in no doubt as to the presence of a strong U-boat pack. The laden merchant ships of the convoy columns were the visible evidence of his huge responsibility.
>
> One patrolling aircraft that evening could have put down every one of these U-boats but, alas, this was the Air Gap and the powers that be had yet to allocate a single V.L.R. [Very Long Range] aircraft to this part of the North Atlantic.[1]

---

[1] Martin Middlebrook, *Convoy: the Battle for Convoys SC.122 and HX.229*, Harmondsworth, 1978, p. 167, lines 11–40. This and further other short extracts are

A NORTH ATLANTIC CONVOY

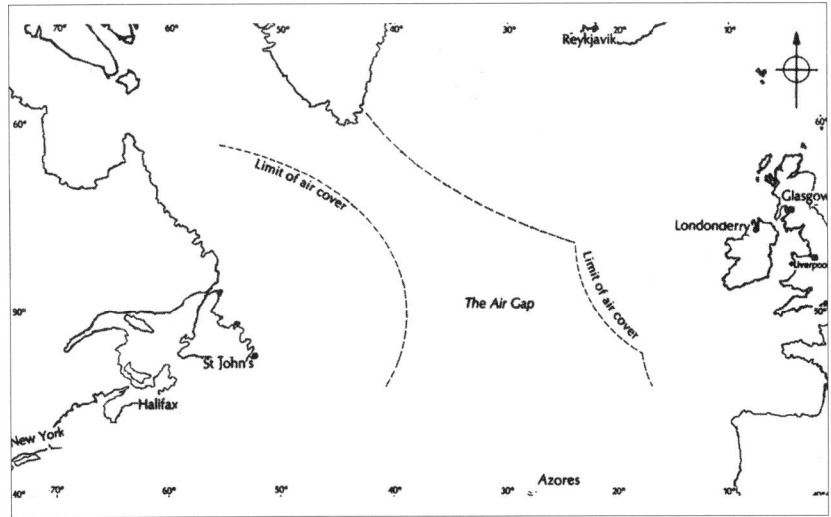

Chart showing the air gap.

The first ship to be torpedoed was a Norwegian, the *Elen K,* which sank very quickly but not before she had carried out the standard 'torpedoed ship' routine by lighting the red masthead light, sounding four blasts on her siren, and firing two distress rockets. The order to abandon ship was given which the crew, being experienced, disciplined and well trained, did so in orderly fashion and all were rescued. During the next three hours three more ships were sunk.

> From *Volunteer*'s bridge, Lieutenant-Commander Luther had seen the second of *Elen K*'s distress rockets but he was not even sure that a ship had been torpedoed at all; he had seen no explosion and the *Elen K* had sunk so fast that no ship had been seen dropping astern of the convoy. Luther ordered the standard move for moonlit conditions known as Half Raspberry in which all escorts turned outwards and swept their own sector with radar and Asdic but without using starshell. The four escorts carried out the manoeuvre but without any U-boat being detected.[2]

reproduced by permission of Penguin Books Ltd.
[2] Asdic is the acronym for 'Anti-Submarine Detection Investigation Committee'.

For the next hour all was quiet; then, the Dutch merchant ship *Zaanland* was hit, followed almost immediately by the *James Oglethorpe*, an American Liberty ship. The captain of the *Zaanland,* seeing she was sinking rapidly, ordered the crew to abandon ship, which they did and, as with the *Elen K*, in good seaman-like order. The captain of the *Zaanland* was the last to leave the ship and he fell into the sea as he tried to get into the last lifeboat. He was almost drowned, being soaked in fuel oil, but by a lucky chance one of the lifeboats picked him up and all of the crew were eventually saved.

Those in the *James Oglethorpe* were not so fortunate; half of the crew abandoned ship and were rescued; the others, including the captain, stayed with the damaged ship and tried to return to St John's. Nothing more was ever heard of her or her depleted crew and it was thought that she sank and they were all drowned.

Another Half Raspberry was ordered. The corvette *Anemone* spotted a U-boat on the surface as she was performing the Half Raspberry and thundered after it. The U-boat crash dived and *Anemone* dropped depth charges over the spot where she had dived. *Anemone* continued to chase the submarine dropping depth charges as she made Asdic or radar contacts whenever the submarine reappeared. It was a long chase and, after attacking the U-boat for the fifth time, no further contact or sighting was made and *Anemone* returned to the convoy; she had been away for some two hours.

> Lieutenant-Commander Luther had been kept touch about the progress of *Anemone*'s depth-charge attack but there had been no question of sending another escort to join in the action because for some time *Volunteer* had been the only escort remaining with the convoy. After finishing his own Half Raspberry manoeuvre, Luther decided to sweep across the rear of the convoy. To his intense dismay, Luther found yet another merchant ship listing heavily to starboard and blowing off steam. Its crew was taking to their lifeboats. This ship was another of the convoy's American Liberty ships, the *William Eustis*, also on its first voyage.... There was no point in Luther ordering any more Half Raspberries for the non-existent escort and he was now left with the difficult choice of hunting for the attacking U-boat himself, staying to protect the convoy from further attacks, or stopping to pick up the American crew – the last ship in the column had again failed to stop.... *Volunteer*'s captain did not take long to reach a decision. The destroyer made a wide Asdic sweep around the wrecked Liberty ship in case a U-boat was nearby, then slowed down to start picking up the American

A NORTH ATLANTIC CONVOY

*Dashing off at high speed after dropping a depth charge.
(Photo from Terry Simpson)*

seamen.[3]

Two of the *William Eustis*'s boats had been smashed by the torpedo explosion but the entire crew had got away in the remaining four boats and on the life rafts.

The crew of *Volunteer* must have been nearly exhausted, busily picking up survivors from the *William Eustis*. They were still on action stations with all that entailed, having no chance of food, rest, or sleep. It did not help when it was then discovered that the code-books and other confidential papers from the *William Eustis* had not been dumped.

> We went very fast past her and fired four depth charges from the throwers as we went by. They all exploded underneath her and lifted her about five feet out of the water – it was quite a dramatic sight. We went whizzing back to the convoy. The survivors told us she had been carrying 7,000 tons of sugar. Later we worked out how many cups of tea that sugar would have made and were horrified to think we had just

[3] Middlebrook, *op. cit.*, p. 181, lines 19–29 and 35–9, p. 182, lines 8–14.

sunk about three weeks' sugar ration for Britain. (Lieutenant G. C. Leslie).[4]

Midnight passed and St Patrick's day, 17 March, was heralded, at 0045 hours, with the sinking of another ship, the *Harry Luckenbach*. She was torpedoed and sank within four minutes and a number of the crew was killed instantly by the explosion. The lifeboats with the surviving crew were never picked up or heard of again. The whole crew of fifty-four merchant seamen and twenty-six naval men were lost.

Some few hours passed with little happening: then more explosions, the sounding of sirens, distress rockets and red lighted mastheads were heard and seen. This time three ships had been hit: *Irénée du Pont,* an American freighter, the British refrigerated ship, *Nariva,* and the *Southern Princess*, a British tanker of 12,156 tons and the largest ship in the convoy.

The *Irénée du Pont*, the first to be hit, was struck with two torpedoes and there was a bit of a panic. A number of the crew dived into the water and only two lifeboats were launched. Thirteen of *Irénée du Pont*'s crew were lost.

> The second ship to be hit was the *Nariva*. Second Officer G. D. Williams was on duty at the time. 'Nariva was torpedoed with an ear-shattering roar and the deck bucked and heaved violently under my feet. A huge tower of black smoke, tons of water and debris was flung into the air just forward of the bridge. Captain Dodds came out on to the port wing of the bridge when I remembered the adage that what goes up must just as assuredly come down and, without ceremony, I pushed the "old man" back into the wheel-house and not a second too soon for tons of water and debris fell on the bridge with a crunch and clatter. . . . The ship was making water fast and the forward welldeck was soon awash. The order was given to abandon ship and the boats launched.'[5]

All the crew of the *Nariva* survived.

> The third ship hit in this attack was the *Southern Princess*, a thirty-year-old tanker (previously named *San Patricio*) which had once been converted to become a whaling factory ship in the Antarctic but was now being used as a tanker again. At 12,156 tons she was easily the largest ship in the convoy, and was carrying 10,000 tons of fuel oil in her cargo tanks and two railway engines and several invasion

---

[4] Middlebrook, *op. cit.*, p. 182, lines 41–4 and p. 183, lines 1–4.
[5] *ibid.*, p. 189, lines 4–13 and lines 17–19.

barges on the flat whale-flensing deck above the main deck. One torpedo had hit on the starboard side under the bridge, the explosion breaking down the bulkheads between the cargo tanks and the crew accommodation, and the oil was soon flooding into the quarters and also out of the torpedo hole onto the surface of the sea. The explosion ignited the gas in the top of the rear-most cargo tank and the oil in the holds soon caught fire. The resulting huge, towering blaze became so intense that the paintwork on a ship in the next column was blistered and onlookers could hear the agonizing screams from men trapped on the forepart of the *Southern Princess*. They feared there would be a huge loss of life – 'We watched in stupefying silence and fascinated horror, hardly believing that it was real.'

The situation on the *Southern Princess* was not as serious as might be imagined . . . Only four of those aboard failed to get away safely – two passengers and two teenage boys.[6]

The reader will remember that Commodore Mayall had instructed that in the event of a ship being torpedoed the last ship in each column was to stop and pick up survivors, but so far no ship had observed this instruction. However there was one ship whose young captain did.

The last ship in the *Irénée du Pont*'s column was the New Zealand Shipping Company's refrigerated ship *Tekoa* with Captain Albert Hocken in his first command as master. Earlier, after he had seen five ships torpedoed nearby and not one merchant ship at the tail of a column had stopped to rescue survivors, Hocken had signalled the Commodore, 'Am I to act as rescue ship without further signal from you?' and received the reply that the order still held. When the *Irénée du Pont* was hit, Captain Hocken immediately gave orders that *Tekoa* was to stop and commence rescuing survivors. The designated rescue ship for *Nariva* and *Southern Princess* did not take the same action.

Lit up by the blazing *Southern Princess*, *Tekoa*'s crew set to work. Rope ladders and cargo nets were lowered over the lee side and lines thrown to the lifeboats which soon came alongside. Many of the *Southern Princess* survivors were covered in oil, and *Tekoa*'s bosun rigged a hosepipe and unceremoniously hosed down each of these as they came aboard. *Mansfield* was detached from the convoy to screen

---

[6] Middlebrook, *Convoy*, p. 189, lines 38–45 and p. 190 lines 1–14 and 16–18.

the rescue work and she also took on board several of the more scattered survivors.[7]

Anemone arrived on the scene and followed suit, rescuing survivors from the *Nariva*. For those on *Pennywort* it must have been a dramatic sight as she passed by, looking for the convoy, with the furiously burning tanker illuminating the scene of rescue. A total of 260 men were rescued.

By early dawn of the 17th their rescue work was finished, so *Tekoa* and *Mansfield* went back to the convoy.

After the convoy with its escorts had resumed its course Lieutenant Commander Luther had the escorts make fast dashes outward from the convoy, sometimes releasing a single depth charge. He hoped this would discourage any U-boat preparing to make a further attack. To the great relief of all no more attacks were made for some few hours.

Then about mid-morning as Commodore Mayall was rearranging the columns in the convoy to fill in the gaps made by the ships that had been sunk, the U-boats attacked again. This time it was the Dutch ship *Terkoelei*. Four lifeboats were launched and the majority of the crew got safely away except for the Lascars. They were in such a state of shock they were unable even to row their lifeboat away from the *Terkoelei* as she went down and a lot of them succumbed in the icy seas.

Almost at once the *Coracero* was hit. A torpedo struck her in the engine room and the men there never stood a chance. All the rest of the crew was rescued.

Performing rescue operations in broad daylight was even more hazardous than at night and no merchant ship had stopped to pick up survivors. Luther therefore had *Volunteer* act as a screen and detailed *Mansfield* to get on with the work of rescue. It took over two hours before the job was completed and both ships rushed back to the convoy dreading what they might find on their return.

Lieutenant Commander Luther was getting desperate and decided he must signal to the Admiralty for help:

> It appeared to me that the time had now come when help must be asked for in the form of reinforcements as, with attacks by day and night and the escorts performing the dual role of escorting and rescue work, there was little hope of saving more than a fraction of the Convoy. Moreover, fuelling had been out of the question due to the weather and

---

[7] Middlebrook, *op. cit.*, p. 190, lines 23–40, p. 190.

the persistent attacks on the Convoy and HMS *Mansfield* was getting very low in both fuel and water. ...The relevant signals read:

'HX.229 ATTACKED, TWO SHIPS TORPEDOED. REQUEST EARLY REINFORCEMENT OF ESCORT. 51.45 NORTH, 32.36 WEST.

HAVE BEVERLEY AND MANSFIELD IN COMPANY, PENNYWORT AND ANENOME OVERTAKING ASTERN. PERSISTENT ATTACKS WILL NOT PERMIT FUELLING AND SITUATION IS BECOMING CRITICAL. D/F AND SIGHTING INDICATES MANY U-BOATS IN CONTACT.'[8]

The Admiralty was unable to send any reinforcements and HX.229 and the escorts would have to battle on alone.

Actually things were improving. *Beverley* had just finished depth charging contacts with U-boats and had so badly damaged one of them that it was unable to take any further part in the battle. She had also made two or even three take fright and lose contact with the convoy. In spite of the situation all the escorts had been harrying the U-boats whenever contacts were made. When Luther got back to the convoy he was mightily relieved to find all was well. By now the convoy was within reach of air cover by the Very Long Range (VLR) aircraft.

The late evening of the 17th March saw the weather worsening with heightening winds and snow squalls and the convoy preparing for another night of conflict with the U-boats. As night fell there were only three escorts with the convoy: the three destroyers, *Volunteer*, *Beverley,* and *Mansfield*. *Volunteer* was put in front of the convoy and at a good speed made sweeps on either side. It was some time later that Luther welcomed the arrival back in the convoy of *Anemone* and *Pennywort*, the two corvettes.

In the early hours of the 18th *Volunteer*'s HF/DF detected a U-boat signal in front of the convoy. She sallied forth on the bearing and although she couldn't find anything dropped a depth charge. This was the only enemy contact that night.

Daylight broke, revealing a hard nor-nor-westerly gale blowing with heavy snow showers. At this point *Mansfield*, unlike *Beverley* who had extra tanks fitted, was running short of fuel and had to leave the convoy. This left HX.229 with only four escorts, but *Highlander* with Commander Day on board was due to join the convoy in the early afternoon.

---

[8] Middlebrook, *op. cit.*, p. 226, lines 37–45 and p. 227, lines 1–9.

Volunteer *swinging round in heavy seas.*
(Photo from Terry Simpson)

The conditions under which *Volunteer* and a tired Luther and crew were experiencing are well described by Martin Middlebrook:

> ... picture a harassed and tired Lieutenant Commander Luther [and his crew including Edgar], working mainly from the open bridge of *Volunteer*, trying to protect his convoy with only four escorts ... in the shrieking, howling gale that brought flurries of snow and caused *Volunteer* to pitch and roll heavily over every wave.[9]

At around 14.00 hours the U-boats struck yet again. This time it was the Canadian Blue Star Line ship *Canadian Star,* a refrigerated ship, hit aft by two torpedoes. At the same time the *Walter Q. Gresham,* a new Liberty ship, received a torpedo, also aft, blowing off the propeller and tearing a great hole in its side. The *Canadian Star* lost thirty souls, including wo- men and children from among the passengers. The *Walter Q. Gresham*'s toll was twenty-seven.

During the rescue operations Commander E. C. L. Day and HMS *Highlander* had finally caught up with the convoy and took over command

---

[9] Middlebrook,*Convoy*, p. 247, lines 8–11 and 13–15.

A NORTH ATLANTIC CONVOY

*Decks awash in heavy weather.
(Photo from Terry Simpson)*

of the escorts; as daylight faded he proceeded to make plans for the night's battle against the U-boats. The heavy burden of responsibility for the whole convoy was no longer on the shoulders of Luther.

Commander Day had hardly taken over command when he was faced with rebellion from the captain of the American merchant ship *Mathew Luckenbach*. He and his crew decided they would be better off sailing on their own as their ship had a speed of 15 knots and the convoy could only do 9 knots. In spite of Commander Day's order to stay, they romped away from the convoy. It turned out to be a fateful decision for the merchant ship; on the following day she was torpedoed and sank. Luckily for them all the crew were rescued.

During the early hours of the next day *Anemone* sighted a U-boat at the back of the convoy; she immediately set off to attack it and *Volunteer* was sent to help. The area around was full of U-boats and for the next hour-and-a-half both ships took part in a fierce and frenzied action. There were so many U-boats around the convoy that the other escorts became involved and by the end of the action no less than seventy depth charges had been dropped and three submarines damaged.

The morning of 19 March showed better weather conditions than had been seen for some days and to further cheer things up the first air patrols over the convoy were being performed. No further attacks on HX.229 were made and the surviving merchant ships and their escorts made safe harbour.

Edgar continued in *Volunteer* on her North Atlantic convoy work until the spring of 1944 when his story continues:

> In late May 1944 we were sent to Portsmouth to escort American landing craft to the Normandy beaches. The harbour and outlying buoys were full with shipping and we were detailed to anchor at a buoy so far from the harbour we felt we were nearer the French coast than Portsmouth. We did a couple of practice runs with the American troops landing on the Isle of Wight. Then we were sent to Falmouth on temporary loan with an American destroyer flotilla that would be escorting American landing craft to the beaches.
>
> We anchored in Carrick Roads off Falmouth and, like Portsmouth, the anchorage was packed with shipping. At first light we were called to action stations and every vessel and shore battery opened fire at some low-flying German aircraft that, we think, were doing a reconnaissance.
>
> A day or two later we received our sealed instructions for Operation NEPTUNE and things got underway. We had not far to go and turned into the river Helford and picked up the American landing craft from a little beach there and formed up with our American flotilla leader and headed for Omaha beach. The Americans we were escorting were on the initial landing force so we pushed forward and the whole armada was sorted out into particular beaches. We stayed in support for quite a long time and were then sent in a hurry to Portsmouth to pick up another wave of American troops and deliver them at first light the next morning. We continued doing this shuttle service with the Americans for about ten days and were then sent to relieve another destroyer that was on anti-submarine patrol further down the Channel.
>
> We then continued with our convoy and U-boat hunting work during the campaign in North West Europe, and at its conclusion in May 1945 I left my old ship after 2½ years of active sea-going service.
>
> It was about a month after D-Day, when on night watch, that I discovered an officer assigned to *Volunteer* was also from Walberswick. He was Antony Cleminson who lived at a house called

'White Barn' and when sharing night watches with him we would often talk about the village and this helped pass the long hours. [See more about Antony Cleminson in HMS *Volunteer* in the tailpiece of this story.]

I was sent to Toronto in Canada to join a newly built Algerine class minesweeper called HMS *Pluto* (not to be confused with the Pipe Line Under the Ocean operation). We returned to the UK to be based at Londonderry, sweeping up our own minefields, which had been laid in the Irish Sea and off the coast of Scotland. When these were clear *Pluto* was based at Stavanger, to clear the German minefields off the coast of Norway. Once the Admiralty was satisfied that all the sea mines had been cleared *Pluto* was paid off and I was sent to Hong Kong to join HMS *Constance*, another destroyer.

Edgar in formal uniform when in Malta after the war. (Photo from Edgar English)

Although the war was over, there was still fighting in Malaya and we were still on a wartime footing patrolling the coast, stopping and searching ships and junks for illegal arms-carrying. The Nationalist Chinese were fighting the Communist Chinese and HMS *Constance* was carrying out the duties of guard ship in both Nanking and Shanghai in case any British people needed to be evacuated in a hurry. This was the time when HMS *Amethyst* was shelled and ran aground on the banks of the Yangtze on her way to Nanking. It entailed a lot of patrol work in the lower reaches and mouth of the Yangtze until the *Amethyst* escaped after I think exactly 100 days. It was on a Sunday afternoon and *Amethyst* was met by several naval ships and the Royal Marine Band of HMS *Belfast*, playing what was then a very popular song, *Cruising down the river on a Sunday afternoon*.

I then left Hong Kong to return home on 25 June 1950, the day the Korean War started. So that was one I missed.

Edgar was demobbed in 1964 and left the Service with the rank of Chief Yeoman of Signals having served his 22 years. He married Beryl Martin in 1958 and they had two children, Linda and Janet, and four grandchildren, two boys and two girls. After leaving the navy Edgar took a job as a postman and soon passed the exam to become a Post Office Counter Clerk at the Head Post Office in Ipswich. He progressed steadily from counter clerk to working behind the scenes sending out cash and stock to sub-Post Offices within the area and he retired in 1989.

It is with extreme sadness that we must end this story by recording the death of Edgar Alfred English who slipped his anchor on All Souls Day, 2

Edgar's and Beryl's wedding: outside Covehithe church.
(Photo from Beryl English)

November 2000, aged 76. The funeral was held at the Ipswich Crematorium on Monday, 13 November 2000. It was a beautiful sunny autumn day and some 200 people attended. This short extract from the eulogy, composed and read by Mr John Allport who also conducted the funeral service, summed up Edgar, the man:

> The Royal Navy is and always will be for this Island Nation 'The Senior Service' and the most respected man in the Royal Navy, by everyone from Junior Artificer in Boy Service to Admiral of the Fleet, is the Chief Petty Officer, addressed on board as 'Chief'. In Edgar we knew the epitome of all you could hope for in a 'Chief' a God-fearing, rock-solid, professional, and courageous man to the end.

Life aboard the convoy ships

Arthur Sharman writes:

At Edgar's funeral I met a number of his shipmates and afterwards one of them wrote to me describing life on board HMS *Volunteer*, which helps to understand the conditions under which these gallant sailors engaged in Atlantic convoys existed. His friend wrote the following:

> The V and W destroyers were designed and built towards the end of the First World War and for several years afterwards. They were planned as high-speed fleet escorts of a battle fleet (battleships, cruisers etc.) preferably for use in home waters or the Mediterranean, certainly not for North Atlantic crossings.
>
> Their main armament was 4 .7" guns and a set of torpedo tubes for high speed attack on enemy warships and depth charge equipment against submarines. They were long and narrow with a short high fo'c'sle and a long low after deck. They were designed for speed and manoeuvrability and had a shallow draught. A number of the V and Ws were modified to give them greater range and additional anti-aircraft defence, which, in theory, enabled the ship to cross the Atlantic without refuelling. Frequently, though, because of tactical manoeuvring, there was a need to refuel from one of the tankers in the convoy, which in a gale presented certain difficulties.
>
> HMS *Volunteer* was designed to have a complement of around 95; we had a crew of about 189. The obvious increases in the crew were because of things not known about in 1917 when she was built, like advanced asdic, radar, HF/DF, coding and anti-aircraft guns. Every

extra man for a new or specialist job meant we had to find extra sleeping space. So we improvised. When you joined the ship you were given a place on one of the inboard lockers normally used to sit on when eating at table. You could sleep there, preferably with one arm round a stanchion; this stopped you falling off on to the deck when the ship rolled. When a member of the messdeck left the ship – was drafted, died, killed, or promoted – you transferred to the table; this was better because it had sides and you couldn't fall off. Next you transferred to the outboard lockers which was even better, being wider than the 18 inches of the inboard locker and between the ship's side and table so you couldn't fall off. Then bliss, you transferred to a hammock sling – you had made it.

Ablutions

There were no showers and no baths. There was a narrow space just inside the fo'c'sle watertight doors next to the galley. Inside this were the heads (the lavatories), narrow steel compartments with a water closet and pump – no doors. Opposite the heads was a long narrow trough with holes in it. At the end was a stack of bowls wedged in. Next to this was a boiler with a tap at the bottom. To wash, shave, bathe, or whatever else you had in mind, you took a bowl, put it under the tap, filled it with, always boiling, water, staggered to a hole in the trough, put it in, cooled down the water from a cold tap above the hole and there you were.

There were minor inconveniences, of course. Being next to the fo'c'sle doors with a following sea the odd wave would wash in over the foot of the door space and you would have your legs washed – for free. This could on occasion be dangerous, if the odd wave was high, you could be swept off your feet, and in fact two matelots had their heads bashed in on the deck head.

Laundry

There was no laundry so when necessary you would have a dhobi day. With a piece of pusser's soap and a bucket and the ever-boiling water, you were in business. Grab a scrubbing brush and you could do a hammock, if you could find a space on the upper deck, in harbour, of course.

Drying? Well, Jimmy the One was not over enthusiastic about dressing the ship overall in vests and pants so we had our own dryer. A couple of ropes in the engine room; the stokers didn't like it but we bribed them with 'gulpers'. 'Gulpers' as opposed to 'sippers' of your rum ration.

Food, drink, and clothing

The Admiralty added a small sum of money to your daily pay towards the cost of clothing called Kit Upkeep Allowance (K.U.A.). You could buy anything from a toothbrush to a uniform at 'Slops' in the Depot, a big ship, if in company, or from a naval tailor in Chatham, Pompey, Plymouth, or Devonport (GUZ). These tailors specialised in 'tiddley' suits – suits which skated round the edges of the official pusser's issue i.e. low cut fronts, wide bell bottoms, and special bows for the black silk.

If you were short of any item of your official clothing at kit inspection you either had to buy it at once or have it issued to you and your pay docked – sometimes resulting in a 'north-easter' when pay day came round.

The Admiralty also allocated a daily sum of money for feeding every officer and rating. In the big ships General Messing was the method adopted. All ratings were fed three meals a day to a weekly menu, all the food being drawn from the ship's stores in bulk; thus every mess had the same meal.

In small ships the preferred method was Victualling Allowance messing. The ship carried large stocks of refrigerated food, dry and tinned goods. There was in every ship of the fleet, large and small, a NAAFI manager with his own storeroom. He supplied many of the items, which the Admiralty did not provide. In all ships of the Fleet, the NAAFI manager formed part of the crew, was uniformed and had the status of a Petty Officer. On board *Volunteer* his shop was about the size of a large settee from which he dispensed your free tobacco ration plus additional tobacco, cigarettes, pipe tobacco, and leaf – all duty free. If you were lucky he also stocked chocolate, sweets and, very rarely, slices of cake. Your 'cook of the mess' could buy on tick whatever his messmates needed for their daily meals. All food drawn from the ships was at an Admiralty fixed price (and very cheap) and the NAAFI manager's prices were equally cut-price.

Each Mess of perhaps 25 men, seated on benches either side of a table fixed to the deck and divided into 3 watches, appointed a 'cook of the mess'. He drew from the stores and from the NAAFI what he needed to prepare meals for the week, took the dishes etc. to the galley where the ship's cook did nothing but cook it in the electric and steam ovens. Before the watches changed the familiar Bo'sun's call sounded over the tannoy: 'Cooks of the mess to the galley' – to collect what they hoped their messmates would enjoy eating. Puddings were usually a 'Clacker', a pastry covered in jam or whatever – or, if you were a budding chef in your watch, perhaps a currant duff. The standards of cuisine varied considerably depending on the skills of the preparer – from tolerable to totally inedible – but we learned. At the end of the month what had been bought for the mess from the ship's stores and the NAAFI was totted up, set against the Admiralty's allowance for the men in the mess and a cash settlement made by the cook of the mess – very often a sum of money to be shared equally among the cook's messmates and sometimes a case of passing the hat round to collect a few bob from each to meet the bill.

Of course there were compensations – Kye was one of the lifesavers. Kye was naval cocoa that came in huge blocks of dark chocolate with lumps of white fat in it. You scraped it into a fanny, poured the ever boiling water on it, stirred it over heat into a thick glutinous black mass, added lashings of sugar and, if you were lucky, generous helpings of your bottled rum ration. The ever-present help in a time of trouble.

Antony Cleminson's Tailpiece

Antony Cleminson's connection with Walberswick goes back to 1928 when his father H. M. Cleminson bought White Barn in Leverett's Lane. He had a yacht on the river Blyth and Antony would spend the Easter and summer holidays there being taught how to handle it. With his brother and his father he was taught about the ways and rules of the sea by a 'Captain' George English. 'Captain' George English came from a different English family from that of Edgar.

The following story about *Volunteer,* though not of chasing about after U-boats, reveals what goes on behind the scenes of activity and makes a pleasant change from all the drama of fear and lost lives described earlier.

ANTONY CLEMINSON'S TAILPIECE

Antony Cleminson writes about his time whilst in HMS *Volunteer*.

I feel incredibly lucky that I suffered no such experiences as Edgar English did in the war. As a regular, one was moved roughly every six months passing the job on to a reservist. Of the seven ships I served in during the war only the first, the cruiser HMS *Devonshire* and the last, the destroyer HMS *Volunteer*, survived the war. My timing was fortunate indeed – the others were all lost after I left them.

Apart from the totally peaceful time in *Volunteer* from July '44 to mid '45 the only convoy work I was involved in was an outward bound Sierra Leone convoy followed by an equally peaceful and leisurely inward return where we were the Escort Leader in HMS *Ibis*.

I joined *Volunteer* about a month after D-Day and left soon after VE Day to join HMS *Wilton* (Hunt Type 2) to go to the Pacific Fleet. On our way to Simonstown for a quick refit the war ended and after an extended refit we came home.

I do well remember sharing night watches with Edgar in *Volunteer* and his name immediately meant Walberswick to me.

The only battle I had whilst in *Volunteer* was with the Victual Office in Portsmouth, which I'm proud to say I won.

If you were in dockyard in Portsmouth under refit you were supplied with delicious white bread from the local contractor, Campions. If you were in Spithead bringing convoys down channel for six or seven days you were supplied with grey bread baked in an Army bakery to meet the extra demand.

The Army bread went hard and mouldy after a day at sea whereas the Campion bread remained delicious and eatable for a week. So I took a washing bag full of samples of day-old and week-old bread from Campions and the Army and said to the committee of Victual Officers, 'Take, eat...' They tasted the week-old Army bread and started to tell me that we didn't store it properly at sea – 'bread should be stored with 3 inches between each loaf', so I said, 'Where in the confines of a destroyer can one find that kind of space?'

Result: *Volunteer* always got Campion bread whether in Dockyard or at Spithead. I never knew if the rest of the seagoing ships were equally favoured.

THE ROYAL NAVY

He was also in *Volunteer*

> ...when after months of inactivity, we test fired the 'Hedgehog'.[10] 23 bombs went their way but the 24th stayed put ... but after a short pause it decided to move after all and went off with a puff rather than a bang and landed, seemingly, on the bows in front of the pom-pom. There was much relief when the coxswain and I found that it had, after all, gone just over the side.

Antony is retired and now lives in London. He is always pleased to receive news of Walberswick and of people he knew when he lived there.

Hedgehog anti-submarine device fitted on Volunteer.
(Photo from Terry Simpson)

---

[10] An anti-submarine device, which could launch 24 bombs in an oval pattern ahead of an escort ship, reducing a U-boat's chance of taking avoiding action.

Recruit Robert English, 5th back row, with other recruits and instructors at Chatham 1935. (Photo from Joyce Thewlis)

Another Royal Navy Tale
Robert Charles English

Robert (Bob) Charles English was born in Walberswick on 1 March 1915. He was the first child of Herbert and 'Queenie' English. He went to school in Walberswick until he was 14 years old, and then was employed as a milk roundsman. On 11 June 1935 he joined the Royal Navy and did his training at Chatham, passing out as a Stoker 2nd Class on the shore establishment HMS *Pembroke* and a year later while serving in HMS *Orion* became Stoker 1st Class.

Bob was serving in the cruiser HMS *Sussex* when war broke out and until 21 September 1940; on 18 October 1940 he was posted back to HMS *Pembroke*. He was then seconded to the cruiser HMS *London*, which was in Chatham dockyard where she had been undergoing large repairs since March 1939. We can but presume that he was, with the rest of the crew, readying the ship for service and undergoing sea trials, because he was then posted to HMS *London* on the same day, 7 February 1941, that the ship was commissioned for service in the Home Fleet. She was under the command of Captain R. M. Servaes, RN, who had joined her in the dockyard the same month as Bob and he continued to serve in her until 3 November 1943.

HMS *London* took part in many engagements and the following is an extract from an official 'HMS *London*, Summary of Service' during the time Bob served in her:

> At the time of the raid into the North Atlantic of the German battleship *Bismarck* and cruiser *Prinz Eugen*, in May 1941, the *London* was escorting home the SS *Arundel* with evacuees from Gibraltar. She was ordered to leave her and close the enemy. While thus helping to form the net around the enemy ships she did not participate in the actual engagements which resulted in the destruction of the *Bismarck*.
>
> On 4 June 1941, however, she intercepted the *Esso Hamburg*, and on 5 June the *Egerland*, two fuel and supply ships for U-boats who had been working in conjunction with the *Bismarck* and *Prinz Eugen*. The *Esso Hamburg* scuttled herself and the *Egerland* was sunk by the destroyer *Brilliant*.
>
> On 21 June 1941, HMS *London* intercepted the German motor vessel *Babitonge*, which had left Santos, Brazil, on 24 April for Brest. This ship had been working with a German armed merchant raider, and was disguised as the Dutch *Japara*. On being intercepted, she scuttled herself, about 930 miles south-west of Freetown.
>
> In September, 1941, the *London* conveyed from Scapa Flow to Archangel the first British and American Missions, headed by Lord Beaverbrook and Mr Averell Harriman, to go to Moscow after the entry of Russia into the War. She also brought home these Missions in October after the Three-Power Conference.

HMS *London* then took part in the escort of convoys to and from north Russia and in different operations of the Home Fleet.

Bob was serving in HMS *London* when she along with three other cruisers and three destroyers made up the covering force for the ill-fated Arctic convoy, PQ.17, which had sailed on 27 June 1942 from Hvalfiord, Iceland. This convoy consisted of 35 merchant ships, three rescue ships and two fleet tankers escorted by six destroyers, four corvettes, three minesweepers, four armed trawlers, and two anti-aircraft ships – quite a formidable escort. In addition a large part of the Home Fleet was giving further support in the way of two capital ships, one aircraft carrier, two cruisers, and more destroyers. Also involved were British, Free French, and Russian submarines.

The reason for this massive gathering of allied naval power was in response to decoded German messages and other reports showing that the Germans intended to attack the convoy with their battleship *Tirpitz*, many other warships and with aircraft. Convoy PQ.17 was carrying much needed war materials for the Russians. The convoy sailed and during the next few days attacks were made on it by a number of aircraft. Five of those aircraft were shot down and the convoy lost two ships, one was sunk and the other abandoned. The Naval Staff in London were getting nervous because they were getting no intelligence about what the German naval forces were up to. The Admiralty sent one message telling the convoy to disperse but then confused the issue by following this up with another message telling it to scatter. This left the convoy to the mercy of the U-boats and aircraft, resulting in the sinking of 24 of the 35 merchant ships in the convoy – a disastrous outcome.

The other ships Bob served in were HMS *Braganza, Highflyer, Bambara, Terror, Sultan,* and *Wildfire*.

It was while he was serving in HMS *London* on the river Tyne that he met a young Geordie lass, Kathy, his future wife. To his shipmates he was always called 'Jerry' and it was not until the actual wedding ceremony that Kathy knew his proper name was Robert Charles. HMS *London* was also on the Tyne when his daughter Joyce was born.

Bob and Kathy with baby daughter Joyce. (Photo from Joyce Thewlis)

Bob must have been very popular with his shipmates, for practically the whole ship's company went to the hospital to see the new baby, much to the consternation of the nursing staff.

One time when his ship was docked in New York and Bob was on shore leave he and another mate got so drunk that they both missed the ship, a serious offence. They were staggering down Fifth Avenue about 5 a.m. with mouths so dry they thought 'the cat had died in them' (Bob's own words) and noticed the milkman had kindly delivered bottles of milk outside one of the most exclusive department stores. They couldn't resist the temptation but Bob, always honest, counted out all the change they had in their pockets. They decided it was enough to pay for the milk, so they deposited the pile of coins on the pavement and proceeded to assuage their thirst. Suddenly a huge hand fell on their shoulders and they found themselves looking into the face of a very large uniformed New York policeman. Bob was relieved that they had paid for the milk first, so the charge of theft did not arise. Because of this escapade, though, Bob lost his Good Conduct badge and the money that came with it. His wife never knew about this incident as her allowance was made up by Bob's making an additional voluntary contribution to her allowance. Six months later his badge and the additional money were restored.

Bob left the Royal Navy in 1957 after 22 years of loyal service as a Chief Engineering Mechanic and settled down in South Shields. He started his civilian life working for a chemical factory in Jarrow. Kathy, who was not in very good health, died in 1974 at the comparatively young age of 54 and Bob took early retirement in 1976.

He then moved to Newton Aycliffe near Darlington where Joyce and her husband and children lived. Eventually he had to move into sheltered accommodation for ex-Service people where he made many friends and became the welfare officer for the local Royal Naval Association.

His daughter and family moved to South Africa and settled in Cape Town and in 1982 Bob spent Christmas and New Year with them. He revisited many of the places he had been during the war including the 'Nelson Pub' in Simonstown which, he told Joyce, 'hasn't changed a bit since the last time I was thrown out of it'. He recalled a very famous Great Dane dog named 'Just Nuisance'. Apparently he befriended all the sailors and would travel on the train with them and make sure they got back to the dockyard safely if they were the worse for wear. There is a bronze statue of him wearing a sailor's hat in the square at Simonstown. It is said they gave him a doggie

ANOTHER ROYAL NAVY TALE

*Bob (back row left) and mates with large doll (front row on left) he bought for Joyce when in Malta.
(Photo from Joyce Thewlis)*

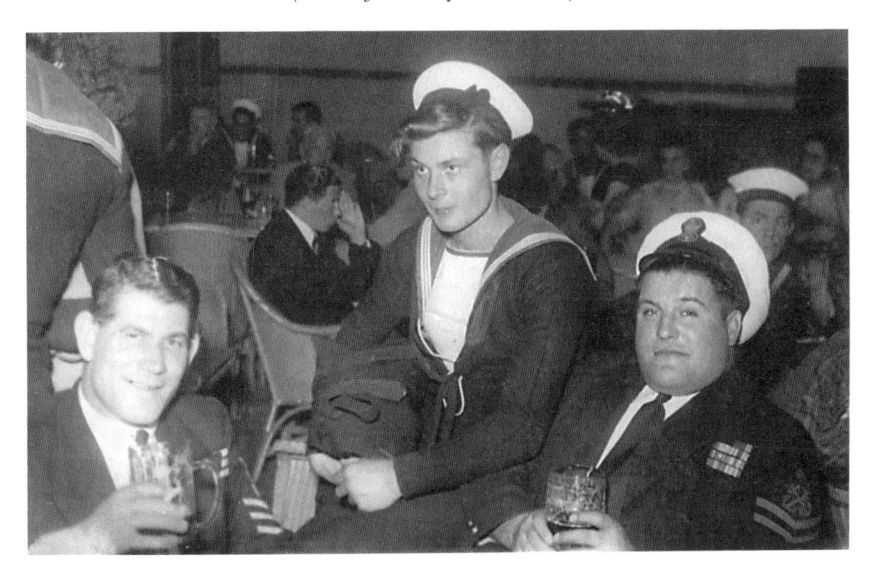

*Bob and shipmates having a convivial evening in a canteen.
(Photo from Joyce Thewlis)*

The frigate Loch Alvie *in which Bob sailed when he went to Malta in 1955.*
(Photo from Joyce Thewlis)

military funeral when he died.

Bob had decided to emigrate to South Africa to spend his last years with his devoted daughter but sadly died of a heart attack in the Royal Navy Club on 20 August 1984 before he was able to leave.

His funeral service was held in the Neville Parade Methodist Church in Newton Aycliffe with all the men from the Royal Naval Association and the Navy Club attending, carrying banners and sounding the Last Post and Reveille. It was a fitting send-off for a loyal and long serving sailor of the Royal Navy.

At Sea

John Oxley Atherton's war

John Oxley Atherton had a house built in Walberswick in 1963 and came to live there in January 1964. Sadly he died on 23 November 1995 before we were able to record his story first-hand. After the war he worked at the atomic power station in Bradwell, Essex, and left there to form part of the team commissioning the Sizewell 'A' Magnox atomic power station. At the time Sizewell 'A' was the largest atomic powered turbine generator in the country. Power from the station was first fed into the national grid in 1966.

His nephew, David Smith, provided the following story about John Atherton. There can be no doubt that there is a lot more to his story than the compilers have been able to gather as the photographs shown at the end of his story indicate.

> John joined the Royal Navy in 1942 at the age of 17 to begin a highly eventful wartime career which was to take him from America, to the D-Day landings, and finally to Burma, Singapore, and the fall of Japan.
>
> He enlisted at Barnsley and did his training at Rothesay. After training at Rothesay as an engineer, John was destined to spend the rest of the war in the cramped, harsh conditions of the engine rooms of some of the Navy's smallest ships. Immediately after training, he was sent to the USA to collect Motor Torpedo Boats (MTBs) which were provided as part of the Lend Lease scheme. Although training in the USA was a welcome break from the rigours of wartime England, the return crossing of the Atlantic in such small ships was extremely risky. John recalled many hours in knee-deep water in the engine room ensuring the pumps could cope with water taken on board during rough weather. Indeed, John was fortunate to survive the crossing as the MTB from which he had only recently been transferred was torpedoed in mid Atlantic.
>
> He arrived back in the UK in time for the preparations for the D-Day landings and took part in several reconnaissance missions to the landing beaches prior to the invasion.
>
> D-Day was an unforgettable experience. He

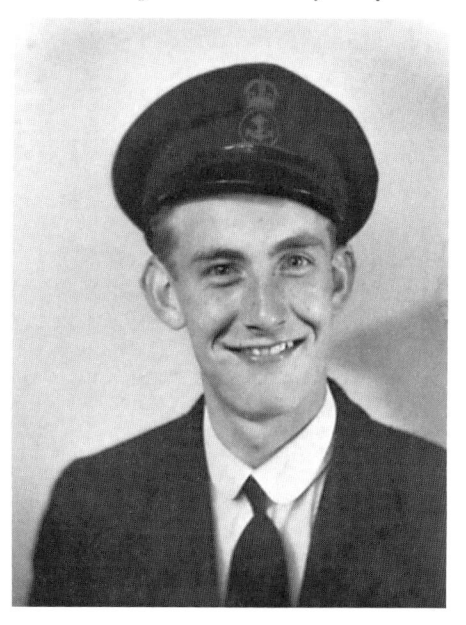

John Atherton, shortly after he enlisted. (Photo from Patricia Atherton)

witnessed the death of his friend from training days, killed by a mine which destroyed the Landing Craft just in front of his, and he often voiced his admiration for the bravery of the troops who had to face the hell of the beaches after being dropped ashore. John was to experience this at first hand when his Landing Craft was stranded on Juno Beach after being put out of action. He vividly recalls a Brigadier Beach Master who paraded up and down the beach playing the bagpipes accompanied by his dog. John spent several days ashore inland from the beachhead sheltering in a house of an old French lady before being evacuated back to England in a ship carrying the wounded.

One of the boats John sailed in whilst on Combined Operations along the Burmese coast.
(Landing Craft Infantry (L) 234/384 tons)
(Photo from Patricia Atherton)

Despite this lucky escape, John's war was far from over. In 1945 he was posted to Burma, again to crew a Landing Craft, and the last year of the war was spent patrolling the coastal waters off Burma. During this time, John contracted a nasty bout of malaria, which caused him to lose a great deal of weight and resulted in his being sent on a month's convalescence from Chittagong to Naini-Tal, a hill station in the Himalayas.

On the news of the Japanese surrender in August 1945, the flotilla was sent to Singapore and arrived in time to see the return of Admiral Mountbatten and to be part of the Surrender Ceremony celebrations. However, the VJ Day festivities were short lived as the crew's

AT SEA

*Above: Japanese giving up their arms.
Below: Lord Louis Mountbatten driving through Singapore.
(Photos from Patricia Atherton)*

harrowing task was to assist in the evacuation of recently released prisoners of war, including many women and children. Their pitiful condition as a result of the cruelty of the Japanese left an indelible impression on John, and as a mark of respect, he refused to buy a Japanese car, camera, or TV throughout the remainder of his life.

On returning to the UK in 1946 John was demobilised, having taken part in some of the most momentous events of the war. There can be no doubt that he had 'done his bit'.

Japanese envoys who signed the surrender and boasted a return in 10 years. (Photo from Patricia Atherton)

Medical Memories
Ian Roxburgh

Dr Ian Roxburgh, MB MRCS MRCGP, came to live in Walberswick in 1988. He was the Secretary of the Walberswick and Blythburgh Branch of the Royal British Legion for a number of years and was an active member until his death in 2001. He wrote:

> At the beginning of the War I had just come down from Cambridge. As a medical student I started my clinical work at Hill End Hospital St. Albans, to which a large part of St. Bartholomew's Hospital had been evacuated. By the time of the Blitz I was back at Barts in London and helped to man a First Aid Post in the City (Aldermanbury). Senior students at Barts were sent to Friern Hospital, Barnet (Colney Hatch) and at this stage I lived at home in Hampstead and went to the hospital by trolley-bus or on my bike. On qualification I returned to Hill End to do a house-job. Penicillin was just being introduced for treatment at this time and small supplies, rather impure, were made available to Barts for clinical trials. After six months the Medical Research Council took me on, as 'Penicillin Officer' at Hill End and it was my job to supervise and record the treatment of those patients fortunate enough to be accepted for the trials. I remember making local bus journeys to a neighbouring hospital with a small attaché case containing vials of the wonder-drug, also a visit by Sir Alexander Fleming – I remember him as dapper man wearing a bow tie.
>
> I was called up in late 1943 as Probationary Temporary Surgeon-Lieutenant, RNVR. I had heard that the Navy wanted someone who knew something about penicillin. I went first to RN Barracks, Portsmouth where as recruits we did a bit of 'square bashing' and learnt how to be an officer ('If you want some gin just press the button for a Steward'). We dined every evening in a semi-darkened hall under an illuminated portrait of Nelson. After a month or so I was drafted to RN Hospital Haslar, at Gosport. Such expertise as I had on penicillin was not apparently needed and I spent most of my time in the Pathology Laboratory, which was run by an amusing Surgeon-Commander from Yorkshire. Life in the Officer's Mess was comfortable and in the early part of 1944 we indulged ourselves in our spare time with Spanish lessons from the RC Padre and 'runs ashore' to the officer's club in Southsea. All this changed however from

D-Day onwards when we received many casualties from Normandy. Less severe cases were transferred onwards to inland hospitals and the more severe we treated at Haslar. I was glad to be back on clinical duties although I had to function also as an anaesthetist. Anaesthetics had not figured prominently in my training; I think I became quite proficient, however, in the end.

In November 1944 I was drafted again, this time to Sydney. We were to organise a hospital to serve the British Pacific Fleet. We sailed out through Panama in a troopship known to us only as 'J1'. She had been one of the Canadian Pacific 'Empresses'. I will always remember the time after years of blackout of seeing the myriad lights of Sydney from the Pacific as we approached. We berthed at Wooloomooloo and spent the first few days based on a small building on the north shore by the Harbour Bridge, pending the arrival of basic supplies for the hospital. This was at Herne Bay, on the Georges River, just south of Sydney and was an enormous hutted hospital, which had been built by the Americans who had now moved north to New Guinea. The whole place had to be totally refurnished with our own equipment. The Australians were really delighted to see us. I think there was a feeling that we had somewhat neglected them during our preoccupation with Hitler in Europe.

Work in the hospital built up steadily and it was a very enjoyable time. Our long-term purpose was to function as a Base Hospital during the anticipated invasion of Japan. I shall never forget a day in August 1945 when we were on leave in the Australian Alps. Our après-ski session in the hotel by a warm log fire was interrupted by someone who said we had dropped a gigantic bomb on Japan. So when the war ended our hospital was gradually run down though we had many ex-POWs from Hong-Kong and Singapore to look after. I returned home in April 1946 and was de-mobbed after a short spell in RN Hospital Stonehouse, Devonport.

Combined Operations
Donald Kett

Donald Albert Kett was born at Blythburgh in 1924, went to the local primary school, and on to Reydon Area Council School. He left school at

COMBINED OPERATIONS

age 14 and went to work at the White House Farm, Bulcamp. As soon as he was old enough, at 17½, in 1941, he enlisted in the Royal Navy, did his initial training, then continued training, and became skilled in handling landing craft. In August 1942 he was on board a landing craft headed towards Dieppe carrying Canadian and British Commandos to the ill-fated Dieppe raid.

Things went badly wrong at the beachhead where Donald landed, for as soon as the landing craft beached he was given a rifle and told to 'Get ashore and help'. The time came for them to return to the landing craft, which was afloat just offshore. He dashed into the water and as he was swimming

Donald in his Royal Navy uniform shortly after enlisting. (Photo from Derek Kett)

towards the ship he was injured in the ankle. However, with great determination he scrambled aboard and eventually arrived back in England. His performance during his foray ashore at Dieppe and the grit and determination shown as he scrambled to get back in the landing craft had been noted. He was just the type of man needed as a Commando in Combined Operations, the organisation under the command of the then Vice Admiral, Lord Louis Mountbatten.

Donald was given the special uniform of half Navy and half Army, which was the Combined Operations uniform, and was sent to the Commando intensive training school in Scotland in readiness for the D-Day landings.

During the D-Day landings Donald received severe shrapnel wounds to his face and head. He was brought back from the Normandy beachhead still clutching his assault weapon and a doubled barreled 12-bore shotgun he had 'won'. He kept the shotgun after he was discharged and, being a keen field sportsman, used it constantly when out shooting.

Donald married a Walberswick girl, Frances Danby, in 1954 and lived there for a number of years. He never really recovered from his wounds; his face was partially paralyzed and the head wound was to cause him much trouble for the rest of his life.

He left Walberswick and lived in Lancashire some time, making only one short visit to Walberswick and another to Blythburgh. He died in 1996 in Lancashire.

Had Donald been alive during the time his story was being compiled he could undoubtedly have given the reader an excellent insight into the life of one of those courageous soldiers: the Combined Operation Commando. Unfortunately, this is all the information that could be gleaned from the memories of Donald's brother Derek and his sister Renée. Derek's and Renée's stories are told elsewhere in this book.

Memories of the war years 50 years on
Robert Stanley

Robert Stanley had a caravan on Ginger Winyard's site next to the beach in Walberswick and has been coming here since 1961. He loved the area, and in 1974 he and his wife Beryl decided they would like to live in the district permanently. They went to Adnams Estate Agents in Southwold looking for a house. It so happened that as they were there a Miss Eileen Peck who lived at 4 Moorside was putting her house up for sale. There was a dearth of suitable houses for sale in the district and Robert and Beryl thought 4 Moorside would be ideal and said they were interested in purchasing the property. They went back to the caravan in Walberswick and spent a worrying night deciding whether they were doing the right thing. Anyway, after much humming and hawing they finally decided to buy it. At the time this meant that Robert would have to commute weekly from London to Walberswick and, although it was a strain at the time, he has never regretted it and has lived there ever since.

His wartime experiences follow:

> The school in Highgate north London was evacuated on the outbreak of war to Westward Ho and with it went our OTC (Officer Training Corps) 'armoury', some 300 long-barrel Lee Enfield rifles and a very old water-cooled Vickers machine gun with its water tank etc. My first experience of war service was to take my turn in guarding this armoury overnight with fixed bayonet. Later the Lee Enfields were replaced by .22 Morris tubed, single-shot breech loading rifles, which we did not

have to guard.

In September 1940 I started on what should have been a four-year course in electrical engineering, two years of theory and two years of practical workshop experience. Before starting the course I joined the Home Guard and, having gained Certificate A in the OTC, was immediately posted to the intelligence section whose only function, as far as I could see, was to follow some map references for a Sunday morning stroll round Edgware. It always ended at the same pub.

Because Faraday House was in the throes of evacuating to south Devon I went straight on to my second practical year at Fielding & Platt, Gloucester, building, among other machines, massive hydraulic presses which formed shell cases. The Gloucester Wagon Works adjoined Field & Platt and between them they had quite an impressive Home Guard which I joined, exchanging my Middlesex cap badge for the two Gloucester badges – one back and one front [the Gloucester Regiment wear two cap badges].

By the time I joined the College in Thurleston, they were well established with an efficient Home Guard; it had to be as we shared the village with a Marine OCTU and they were not playing soldiers when we joined in night exercises with them.

The College moved back to London in 1943. I recall being interviewed, along with the other students in my age group, by a rather tired Major who wanted to know which branch of the services we would like to join. He also sought confirmation from the Principal that we were likely to pass our final exams at the end of the year. I chose the Navy.

Towards the end of the summer those who had chosen the Navy were called to the main Admiralty building in Whitehall for an interview. All very impressive, a large room with a massive boardroom table and a lot of gold braid. I was offered an immediate commission as a Midshipman subject to passing my final exams. Just before Christmas I was able to write to 'My Lords and Commissioners' and to say that I had passed.

Almost by return of post there was a cheque and shopping list – two uniforms, one off the peg, one made to measure, overcoat, shoes, socks, shirts, etc. – also an instruction to report to Portsmouth late on the afternoon of Sunday 9 January 1944. I was to find this was typical of the Navy – never to say where in a town to report.

On the afternoon train to Waterloo there were a number of young men in new uniforms and heavy suitcases and we soon got talking. We were a mixed bag of the professions and all with the same vague instructions.

On arrival at Portsmouth the taxi driver took us to the Wardroom where we were greeted by the Wardroom Master, a fearsome sort of Petty Officer who directed us to the Pier Hotel in Southsea, just a short walk across a park. When we went to pick up our cases we got quite a ticking off – 'Officers do not carry cases, they will be sent over to you at the Pier Hotel'.

At the Pier Hotel all any one seemed to be interested in was taking our ration cards and allocating bunks in cabins on deck; well, we would have to get used to the new terms. We soon found the bar where you could only sign for drinks and then, being Sunday, supper. The spread was a sight for sore eyes after the rationing we had become used to and the service impeccable with, it seemed, two Wrens per officer.

The next morning another surprise. A tap on the door and a Wren called out, 'is everyone in bed?'– and in came mugs of tea and out went our shoes for cleaning.

After a very satisfactory breakfast, the intake for that week, having got together, decided we would go over to the main barracks to see if someone could be found who would take an interest in us. Arriving just on the stroke of nine o'clock we started to cross the main parade ground. This was too much for the training team who rounded us up and we started our ten-day course on how to be a Naval Officer. But first some square bashing, then how to fill in travel warrants, issue rum, and put on gas masks, and other useful things like codes and ciphers. We also attended one Wardroom Dinner, a memorable experience with a Marine Band playing on the balcony, the fine china and plate, and of course trying to get someone to mention a lady's name – the awesome penalty being drinks all round. It was a truly memorable evening and one that was not to be repeated during the rest of my time in the Service.

After ten days at Portsmouth the Electrical Branch officers were given weekend leave and told to report to Roedean, the girls school in Brighton, on the following Monday. Roedean had been taken over by

HMS *Vernon,* the torpedo and the newly created electrical branch (before the war the Navy did not have an Electrical Branch; electrical equipment came under the Torpedo Branch). At Roedean we were given a quick ten-day course on naval electrical equipment and in particular the sweeping of magnetic mines. We were then posted to various ships and establishments.

I was posted to HMS *Cressy*, Dundee, as the second electrical officer. From Dundee we covered both Dundee and Aberdeen bases. Dundee base turned out to be a wooden ship dating back to Nelson's day. It just floated in the dock at high tide but most of the time sat on the bottom. It provided comfortable office accommodation, the Electrical Lieutenant and I each having our own office. We took it in turns to visit Aberdeen on a weekly basis. The base was under control of Rear Admiral Robinson, VC. He had been awarded the VC for action in the Dardanelles in the First World War and had come out of retirement to serve as Commodore Dundee.

The work at Dundee and Aberdeen was not very arduous as we had good teams of Torpedo men well trained in the main job of keeping the fleet of Norwegian whalers at sea sweeping. The Norwegians were amazing as seamen and absolutely dedicated to the task in hand – keeping the North Sea shipping lanes open. Each ship had one British sailor on board and he was usually the Torpedo-man who was trained in the use of the magnetic mine-sweeping gear and, in particular, of the hold full of batteries. These batteries had to be charged each night using the Ford V8 engine which was mounted on deck.

The whalers could only sweep for as long as the battery charge lasted, but this was adequate for the task of keeping the inshore lanes open. I had many enjoyable days at sea with them, joining them for a hearty breakfast and on return to harbour rejoining them in the officers club.

With the exception of the Commodore we were all living ashore in digs. Although I was not qualified as an executive officer, I did help out by taking my turn with the dogwatch to allow the officer of the day to go into town to get his tea. Yes, tea, this was in Scotland. Normally it was very quiet in the dogwatch and I was able to get the paper work out of the way.

In the days leading up to D-Day there was rather more than usual activity and I took the escort to the station to meet the London train and collect the classified documents. The courier was often a Wren Officer who was locked in a compartment and handed the document to us through the window. On this occasion there was one very large parcel for the Commodore which aroused much speculation because it bore the strict instruction that it was not to be opened until instructed to do so. It happened I was on the dogwatch the following day when the WT operator brought me a signal for decoding. In simple terms it said the package could be opened. I shot off to the Commodore's day cabin with the news only to be greeted with, 'Thank you but I have had it open. Come let us have a game of shove halfpenny', a favourite game of his which we often played in the dogwatch. Of course, next morning it was D-Day. I shall never forget how that quite elderly war veteran paced up and down the wardroom sucking his little cherry briar. Oblivious to all around him, he was in spirit with those taking part in the battle being so vividly described on the radio.

In August 1944 my promotion to Electrical Sub-Lieutenant came through. Off came the three brass buttons on the sleeve, which gave rise to the term Snotty for the Midshipmen and also the embarrassment of being mistaken by well-meaning old ladies for the lift boy.

Shortly after my promotion I took a few days leave in Edinburgh, a city I had not previously visited. Whilst there I decided to look up a classmate from the Roedean course. I knew the telephone number but not his address. My telephone call was answered by his chief who

Robert Stanley as a Sub-Lieutenant.
(Photo from Robert Stanley)

informed me, in guarded words, that he was at sea. My response of 'the lucky devil' brought forth enquiries as to what I was currently doing and what made going to sea more attractive. I thought no more of this conversation until a few weeks later when I received instructions to report to Post Box 10, Edinburgh. I did not know the address but, of course, the taxi driver did; it was part of Fettes College taken over by HMS *Vernon* for mine design and mine sweeping. I was greeted with a big grin by the Lieutenant Commander in charge of trials and to whom I had spoken to on the phone. He told me that whilst I was not getting an immediate sea-going appointment it was a step nearer.

I was initiated into the work of the mine-sweeping trials party by Lieutenant Pugh and for a few weeks travelled round the shipyards with him. Our primary task was to run proving trials on the mine sweeping generators of Fleet minesweepers after they had undergone repairs or refits. The worst part of the job was the running of long endurance trials often through the night in some miserable dockyard. Pugh had been with the National Grid before the war and, as we were passing through London on one of our trips, he took me to see the wartime Grid Control Centre which had been moved from Bankside across the Thames to a lift shaft at St Paul's underground railway station. The lift shaft had been turned into a control centre by creating a number of compartments, each separated vertically by ten feet of concrete. The railway tunnels radiating out from the centre of London provided secure routes for the control cables. As far as I know the lift shaft is still there, but the Control Centre moved back to a new building at Bankside.

After just a few weeks at Post Box 10 I was given my first assignment on my own, which was to stand by HMS *Wave,* an Algerine[11] class mine sweeper, which had just been launched at the Lobnitz shipyard at Renfrew on the Clyde. Pre-war Lobnitz were famous for their dredgers and slow speed reciprocating steam engines. It was only a small yard compared with its neighbours on the Clyde but it turned out some first-class work. Alas, today Lobnitz like so many other yards has closed.

The Algerine was the largest of the fleet mine sweepers with a crew of one hundred men and nine or ten officers. When I arrived at Renfrew there were just the First Lieutenant and the Chief Engineer both, like

---

[11] See Edgar English's story, above.

myself, RNVRs. There were also the Coxswain and one or two Petty Officers all regular RNs.

My task was twofold, one to learn all I could about the electrical installation so that I would be able to train the crew when they arrived, and second, to liaise with a Mr Crocker, the Admiralty electrical overseer, in seeing that the equipment was being installed in accordance with the specifications.

At this stage of its construction the ship was not in a fit state to live aboard, so I had to find accommodation ashore and moved into the Officers Club in Glasgow. This was very comfortable; it had been the German Consulate. Gradually the ship took shape. The many specialist items of equipment were arriving all the time and with them more officers and crew. Soon all was complete, and the food was put aboard with the all-important wardroom supplies.

The officers and crew moved aboard and, with representatives of the shipbuilders, we set sail down the Clyde to the measured mile off Rothesay.

When it had been proved that the engines were capable of propelling the ship at 14 knots and each department had reported to the Captain that all was in order, the Captain signed for the ship. A signal was sent to Admiralty and *Wave* became part of the fleet as HMS *Wave*.

HMS Wave. *(Photo from Robert Stanley)*

Following a boiler clean at Port Glasgow and much scrubbing and polishing it was off up the coast and through the Pentland Firth to Granton, the Edinburgh Naval Base. Here we joined seven more Algerines; some had been built at Harland & Wolf in Belfast and others at shipyards in Canada.

Working up the flotilla, now comprising eight mine sweepers and two Dan buoy layers (these were converted trawlers), took some two to three weeks as many of the crew had not been to sea before or had not had experience with mine-sweeping equipment. Apart from the sweeping gear for both moored and magnetic mines, the 4-inch gun and the Oerlikons together with depth charge throwers all had to be tested and the crew trained in their use. At this point the flotilla had eight electrical officers and the quota was two. Six of us made our way back to Post Box 10. Then for me it was off to Lobnitz again to repeat the whole process with HMS *Welcome*. Again I was posted back to the trials party until appointed to the 18th Mine Sweeping flotilla operating out of Parkstone Quay, Harwich.

The spring of 1945 brought with it a lot of work for the minesweepers. First there were the East Coast shipping routes to be swept and then, as the ground forces reached Holland, our attention turned to creating safe channels into Holland. The press at the time very aptly called them 'bread channels into Holland'. For us it was just a question of pounding back and forth, eight abreast, trailing our magnetic mine-sweeping cables. In the event we found very few mines; most of them were in the shallower waters which were being dealt with by the smaller sweepers, the BIMS [British Inshore Mine Sweepers (British Yard motor mine sweepers)] and the BAMS [British American Mine Sweepers (Lend Lease to Great Britain)].

At the end of April the 10th and 18th flotillas joined forces and set sail up the East Coast until we were just off the Humber where we changed course for Cuxhaven and Helgoland Bight area. As we formed line abreast, 16 ships in sweeping configuration, flotillas of the smaller BIMS and BAMS came in behind us, and behind them special mine-sweeping motor torpedo boats; a most impressive sight; a veritable armada. Then came the signal, the war in Europe was over. Splice the main brace. Next morning a German submarine surfaced close on our starboard bow and for a few moments we wondered whether they knew the war was over. They did and all was well.

Just south of Helgoland the Fleet Minesweepers changed station to allow the BIMS and BAMS to take the lead followed by the MTBs (Motor Torpedo Boats). They went on to clear channels into Bremerhaven and Cuxhaven. We did not see them again, as our task was to clear the area south of Helgoland up to the shallower waters off Cuxhaven and Bremerhaven. We were seeking the magnetic mines the RAF had laid at various times. We did not find any, although we were at sea for close on a month before we had a short spell in Cuxhaven to replenish supplies and collect spares. I recall the relief and admiration I had for HMS *Vernon's* organising skills. As we came alongside the quay there was Lieutenant Harry Pickup, later manager of the Yorkshire Electricity Board's Wakefield District, with a desperately needed 8-foot diameter drum of buoyant cable together with other badly needed spares all of which they had brought overland. Some repair work was put out to local firms; and on one occasion, whilst in discussion with the Manager, I noticed that Harry had taken a sudden keen interest in some drawings in the office. The Manager admitted they were connected with work they had been doing on the snorkel submarine-breathing device. Closer questioning brought forth the information that a submarine with trial equipment had been scuttled just before the Allies had arrived. This information was passed on but I do not know what action was taken.

Whilst in Cuxhaven the no fraternising rule was in force and some of the girls thought they could embarrass our troops if they stripped and pranced around on the beach naked. They had not counted on the quick reaction of a naval patrol that sized up the situation and made off with their clothes.

After more weeks of sweeping we returned to Parkstone Quay for a short rest and some intensive maintenance. Then for two ships of the flotilla it was back to Germany to provide an escort for the *Europa* – the German 'Strength through Joy' liner – which the Americans were taking out of Bremerhaven as war reparations. This was not without incident because, although fully briefed as to the changes of course required to stay in the swept channel, they seemed incapable of reading flag signals and the only common radio link was a very poor walkie-talkie. The result was almost a forgone conclusion – they would go the wrong way; they did, and nearly rammed one of the sweepers. The *Europa,* I believe, ended up as the *Isle de France.*

By this time the flotilla was in desperate need of a refit and it was scattered all over the country, London, Chatham, Liverpool, and Ipswich. My home was in Edgware, North London, so with careful planning I passed through London most weekends en route to one or other of the ships.

With the refits completed the flotilla reformed at Harwich and set sail for Cobh in S. Ireland. Cobh used to be known as Queenstown and the nearest town is Cork. We were, I think, the first naval force to visit Cobh since the 'Troubles'. Our reason for being there was to clear the mines we had laid deep outside the harbour to ensure no German submarines could seek shelter or otherwise use Cobh as a base.

We received the warmest of welcomes from the people of Cork. Immediately we were granted honorary membership of the Yacht Club and the Tennis Club and very soon had established a circle of friends among the owners of some of the large stores in Cork and with solicitors, doctors, dentists, and the like and were being invited to join them in their boxes at the theatre and afterwards go back to their homes. It was not unusual for them to loan us a car for the duration of our stay in harbour; this got round the problem of the last train to Cobh. Very soon after our arrival a Mr Maloney made himself known. He was a solicitor by profession and offered his services should we need them. He had served in the RNVR in the First World War and obviously enjoyed wardroom hospitality; we made him an honorary member.

In July 1946 I was promoted to Electrical Lieutenant and, whilst this brought with it an increase in pay for me, the ten days at sea wire sweeping were sheer boredom beyond belief. Much of the late summer was spent, stripped to the waist, scraping Admiralty grey paint off the 12-foot International, which we had as one of the lifeboats, giving it a coat of varnish and generally trying to get it fit for sailing. We put in for one regatta but the sails were very heavy canvases and it easily capsized. It cost me a case of beer for the crew of our duty boats rescue mission.

The actual sweeping was straightforward. We had accurate charts showing where the mines had been laid and the Navigator would be able to forecast, say, ten in this row and then count down. With luck up came ten mines and we sank them with rifle fire, although the Boyes anti-tank .55 rifle was by far the most effective weapon – but with a kick like a mule until we had some proper mountings fitted on the bridge. A mine should render itself safe when cut from its mooring but due to marine growth this did not always happen. If a horn was struck and the safety device had failed the resulting explosion would shower the decks with seaweed and other debris, much to the annoyance of the First Lieutenant. The sweeping problems started when only eight or nine mines came up instead of the ten; we just had to go on pounding back and forth until they were all found. On one occasion we had a very good day, everything went right from the start and we had a bag of one hundred mines.

The four nights in harbour were an ample reward for the ten days at sea even if we did not get much sleep. Typical was the Irish Army Ball. As I could produce a partner I was detailed as the one who would accept the invitation on behalf of the ship. One Officer and one Rating were invited from each ship. The current girl friend could not be ready before nine o'clock but she assured me even at that hour the Ball would hardly have got going. She was right and the army laid on cars about seven next morning.

It was not always roses for the sailors, though, because there was an element who had been fed on a diet of hatred with their mother's milk. This could lead to problems at closing time when a brick would be lobbed through the pub window by youths that would then find the Garda and claim the sailors had been responsible.

There was one incident where the solicitor Maloney earned his keep. Two of my lads had been in a café when it was discovered that money was missing from the till. They were arrested but we came to an arrangement whereby the matter would be dealt with when we returned from our next sweep in ten days time.

The two lads and I caught the train to Cork and were met by Maloney and a bevy of Garda. Whilst some of them took the lads off to the court two of the sergeants had other ideas and started banging on the door of the refreshment room demanding they 'open up in the name of the law'. Several Guinnesses later we arrived at the Court and our case came on. It was real theatre; Maloney was in great form and in next to no time had tied the witnesses in knots. He had one in tears and was told to go easy with another because of a heart condition. The case was thrown out and the two lads, Maloney, the prosecution, and Garda all retired to the nearest bar.

The work of sweeping went on through the late summer and autumn and the only memorable events for me were the tragic loss of a seaman who was paying out the sweep wire and stepped into a loop. In an instant he was dragged overboard and was drowned. Thankfully that was the only death I witnessed during the whole war.

On another occasion we were pulling in the sweep at the end of the day when a mine was spotted caught in the sweep. A moored mine would normally just float to the surface, but this one exploded a short way astern of the ship before it could be cut free. The result was that the impact on the engine caused a crankshaft web to fracture; the engine was a write-off. Admiralty ordered us back to Plymouth to pay off. Fine, but there was a problem. It had been a very hospitable ship with many Irish friends and as I was in charge of the wine account I had found it necessary to have two wine suppliers to ensure adequate stocks. We had just had a delivery and stocks were well over the limit. I went ashore and discussed the problem with the local wine merchant. He could see no problem. We had wines and spirits he could use and he had wines and ports and brandy which was not available to us. The Irish Customs did not bat and eyelid when the wine merchant's man made repeated visits to us with his sack trolley to 'collect empties'.

Just before this incident we had, as a flotilla, put on a dance for our friends from Cork and the locals. The dance was on a Sunday evening and started quite late and in low key until midnight when, as it was no longer Sunday, the bar was able to open. We were due to sail at eight o'clock on the Monday morning but at seven o'clock the crews were still at the dance. Somehow we got everybody back on to their ship and being the Navy, hangovers or not, if we said we were going to sail at a certain time then that was when we sailed.

Once out of the harbour the flotilla Captain found a safe anchorage just off the coast and ordered a party ashore to negotiate with the farmer to use some of his fields for football. As many as possible were put ashore whilst the rest had to 'make do and mend'. There was a prearranged signal for our immediate return if the weather deteriorated. The play was pretty rough and I caught my wrist in a fall. The weather started to change and we were ordered back to our ships and then carried on with ten days of routine sweeping. Back in harbour I went to see the flotilla doctor who could find nothing wrong with my wrist that an aspirin would not put right. It was then back to sea for more sweeping. It was during this sweep that we had to return to Cobh with the damaged ship and prepare for the trip to Plymouth on one engine.

When we arrived in Plymouth I, together with most of the officers and crew, went on leave while it was being decided what to do about the damaged sweeper. I knew that when I had had some leave I would return to the flotilla and a berth would be found for me on another ship. My being moved from ship to ship had happened before, once in the middle of the North Sea.

Whilst on leave my wrist was still weak and painful and I went to the Edgware General Hospital, where an X-ray confirmed a Colles' fracture and my wrist and forearm were encased in plaster.

At the end of my leave I returned to Plymouth to take passage back to the flotilla on one of the Dan buoy layers; but immediately I reported aboard, the Captain said I could not report back from leave sick. I would have to get clearance from the Naval Hospital before he would take me. At the hospital they took an X-ray and put on a new plaster. I was then interviewed by a Surgeon Commander who told me, in no uncertain terms, that the Navy would not countenance my being on a small ship with an arm in plaster because a further accident could raise liability problems. An ambulance would be sent to collect my gear and me from the Dan buoy layer.

The hospital was very comfortable, I had my own room and no restriction on how I should spend the evening as long as I was back by about 10 o'clock. I had a walk round and visited the famous Plymouth Hoe and then back to the hospital where the nurse made up the most wonderful nightcap which seemed to be a mixture of Horlicks and Ovaltine. Next morning we were called, as a bathroom became free, the drill being that those who had been turned out first one day would have a later bath the next day. After breakfast we returned to our rooms and stood at the foot of the bed while the Commander was doing his rounds – seemed to be more interested in whether the under frame of the bed had been dusted than how the patient was. At lunch there was a very welcome bottle of beer for everyone. This was a bequest made by a well-wisher in days long past.

After a further X-ray I was sent on leave and told to report back in eight weeks, this I did and was sent on leave pending reappointment. I thought I would be forgotten until my demob came up in the New Year but no such luck. Within a couple of weeks my demob papers came through, although I did have to visit Queen Anne's Mansions, a part of the Admiralty, for physiotherapy for several weeks until I signed a waiver of any claim for lack of proper medical attention.

Well, that was my war; a holiday compared with the horrors some had to face, but for me a wonderful experience. As a bonus the three years, all but a few days, counted as the fourth year of my Faraday House Diploma Course and was accepted by the IEE (Institution of Electrical Engineers) for corporate membership leading in later years to Fellow.

Chapter 2
THE ARMY

Armoured Warfare (1)
Herbert English

Herbert was born in Walberswick and went to the local village school. In 1931 he passed the Scholarship Examination, and received a secondary education at the Sir John Leman Grammar School at Beccles. His name was only the second one recorded on the Walberswick School Honours Board. Since the school's closure this Honours Board has been preserved and is displayed in the village hall.

He writes:

> I joined the Army as an apprentice in January 1935 and served three years training as a fitter at the Army Technical School at Chepstow, Monmouthshire. Three years later at eighteen, having completed my apprenticeship, I joined the 12th Royal Lancers at Tidworth, Hampshire, as a Squadron Fitter. The 12th Royal Lancers were at that time one of the very few Armoured Car Regiments in the British Army equipped with Lanchesters and a few Rolls Royces. They were quite old vehicles and by the end of 1938 had been replaced by Morris cars.
>
> In late September 1939 we went to France taking our Morris armoured cars equipped with Boyes anti-tank rifles with us. In May 1940 we advanced as far as Louvain in Belgium and then had to retreat in the face of the German panzers.
>
> I remember riding a motor bike when we were advancing to Louvain and going through Brussels where we were greeted with chocolates, flowers and kisses from the females but, understandably I suppose, we had no such welcome when we fell back.
>
> Our armoured vehicles were no match whatsoever for the German tanks and all we could do was to try and take them by surprise. We would conceal ourselves as far as possible and catch them coming round corners or over the crest of a hill. As many rounds as possible would be fired at them and we would then beat a hasty retreat and position ourselves to repeat the performance all over again.

ARMOURED WARFARE (1)

We saw many distressing scenes on our retreat towards Dunkirk but one in particular remains in my memory. We were in Belgium travelling down a long, wide avenue and came across a large number of horses that had been blown to pieces by shrapnel – it was a sickening sight, which I have been unable to forget.

We made our way back to a village called Ghyvelde near the coast, harrying and holding the enemy up as much as possible. It was there that we had to destroy all our vehicles and march back to the outskirts of Dunkirk. We suffered some bombing but luckily had very few casualties. General (Colonel as he was then) Lumsden was in charge of a section of the beach there and we were in the sand dunes for several days watching as hundreds of troops struggled through the water to get on to the waiting ships.

We must have been fairly successful in the part we played in the retreat and evacuation because I remember that after Dunkirk the 12th Royal Lancers had more mentions in the daily press than almost any other regiment.

The lead up to this part of Herbert's story begins on 11 September 1939 when British troops moved to France, and by late September the 12th Royal Lancers, commanded by Colonel (later General) Lumsden were also there. They became part of the 150,000 troops and 24,000 vehicles making up the BEF under the command of General Lord Gort.

On 10 May 1940 the Germans began their successful blitzkrieg against Holland and Belgium. The following day the 12th Royal Lancers with General Montgomery's 3rd Division occupied their position along the line of the river Dyle at Louvain in Belgium. On 14 May, as the Germans swept through Belgium, Montgomery had his first engagement against the enemy Panzers. He succeeded in driving them off, but this action did not stop the German blitzkrieg attack and the BEF soon was in danger of being out-flanked.

Five days later, on 19 May, General Gort reported to London that the French 1st Army front to his east was crumbling. Churchill sent General Sir Edmund Ironside, Chief of the Imperial General Staff (CIGS), to report on the state of affairs. As a result of his report, the British and French troops made an attempt, on 21 May, to stabilise the situation by attacking the Germans at Arras. A fierce nine-hour battle ensued, but when the Germans brought their 88mm artillery and Stukas into the fray the British were forced to retreat. It was this that decided General Gort, on 25 May, to fall back on Dunkirk and call for an evacuation.

Meanwhile, Churchill, on 20 May, had ordered Admiral Ramsey, naval commander at Dover, to assemble a fleet of small craft ready to go to ports and inlets on the French coast to evacuate the retreating troops. The evacuation was called Operation DYNAMO and on 26 May the order was given to proceed. The 12th Royal Lancers with the rest of the Army retreated to Dunkirk and they, with nearly 340,000 British and Allied troops, were evacuated to England.

Herbert takes up the story:

> Upon our Regiment's return to England we were reformed at Hamworthy near Poole, Dorset, and equipped with Beaveretts. These vehicles were made from a Standard saloon car chassis covered with mild steel on both sides and another one on the front with a slot for the driver to see through. They were completely open at the back and on top with no armament whatsoever, but I believe they were equipped with radios. We still had these when we moved to Long Melford, Suffolk, where as a reconnaissance unit we were kept on alert during the invasion scare in the early autumn of 1940.
>
> Our next move was to Rusper in West Sussex where we were billeted in a large country house – Lyne House, the home of the Broadwood family, well-known piano makers. Lyne House was about a half-mile off the main road down a gravel drive. At this time we were being equipped with Humber and Daimler armoured cars, much heavier vehicles than the Beaveretts, and fitted with Boyes anti-tank rifles and machine guns in the turrets. These heavy vehicles soon made a mess of the driveway. This was the time when the Germans were bombing London nightly, so we sent lorries up there to bring back loads of brick rubble to repair the drives. I imagine that some of this rubble is still there.
>
> It was at this time, January 1941, I met a very nice local girl, Joyce Brooking, not quite 17 years old at the time. Her father was the local garage owner. Shortly after our Regiment left Rusper, Joyce joined the Royal Naval Hospital at Haslar in Portsmouth to train as a nurse. On completion of her training she was posted to the Royal Naval Air Station at Dale in South Wales. Later, on 21 September 1944, while she was still at Dale and I was stationed at Farnborough, we were

ARMOURED WARFARE (1)

Herbert and Joyce outside Rusper Parish Church.
(Photo from Herbert English)

married in Rusper church. On 27 April 1946 our daughter Judith was born and on 7 December 1948 we had a son Geoffrey.

We were stationed at Rusper for about eight months and our Regiment was then sent to North Africa via Durban. We advanced through the desert, first with General Wavell to El Agheila then retreated to the Egyptian border. Again we advanced, this time with General Auchinleck, and retreated once again. I was with the 1st Armoured Division on the retreat to Benghazi and after the battle of El Alamein advanced with General Montgomery as far as El Hamma in Tunisia. At El Hamma with the New Zealand Division we got behind the German army by going south into the desert to attack their rear.

The following is a slightly more detailed description of what was going on at that time in North Africa.

Under General Sir Archibald Wavell the 12th Royal Lancers had advanced through the desert to El Agheila but were forced to retreat beyond Bardia to the Egyptian border. Again they advanced, this time with General Auchinleck who had rebuilt the allied forces into a new unit, the Eighth Army. Once again the Lancers had to retreat, but after the battle of El Alamein they advanced under their new commander General Montgomery to Medenine.

At about that time Rommel had retreated from the Kasserine Pass to form his main defence behind the Mareth Line. He planned to attack the British at Medenine, but decoded German messages had forewarned General

THE ARMY

Montgomery of this and the 51st Highland and 7th Armoured Division were ready for them; Rommel's panzers were badly mauled, losing 52 tanks and having almost 700 casualties. General Montgomery then had the 2nd New Zealand Division make a massive 200-mile outflanking movement through very difficult terrain to the El Hamma valley in Tunisia in order to get behind the Mareth Line. Bad weather held things up and a counterattack by the 15th Panzer Division stopped the advance. General Montgomery then switched tactics, sending the 1st Armoured Division after the New Zealanders to deliver a knockout blow. The stony hills and little valleys in the area gave plenty of cover for the German panzers and anti-tank guns, so on 26 March the RAF strafed and bombed the area to allow the New Zealanders to advance. That night, as planned, the 1st Armoured Division passed through the New Zealand lines. The ground there was strewn with rocks and bomb craters so progress was slow. During the night the Germans put a screen of 88mm guns across the entrance to the valley, which held up the advance for two days. Nevertheless this threat to the Germans in the rear of the Mareth Line caused them to fall back to Wadi Akrit and subsequent engagements sent the Axis forces in full retreat towards Tunis and Bizerta.

It was on 27 March that Herbert was caught in the blast of a shell from a German tank and badly wounded. He writes:

> I was flown to Tripoli where I stayed in hospital for about six months and went back to Alexandria on HMHS *Oxfordshire*, a Royal Navy hospital ship, and then on to Cairo. After a few months there I went back to Alexandria and was sent home on an Army hospital ship the *Abba*. This ship in no way compared to the *Oxfordshire* but was a rather dilapidated vessel altogether. I arrived back in Walberswick about a week before Christmas 1943 and had to walk over to Southwold hospital to have my wound dressed daily. In January 1944 I had to go to Ipswich hospital for another operation.

Herbert had already had ten operations when he was in Tripoli; after a period of convalescence he was sent to the 58th Training Regiment at Farnborough to train recruits in tank warfare. He finished his service with the 58th Training Regiment and was demobbed in mid January 1946 with the rank of Staff Sergeant.

He started his civilian life working for a time with his father-in-law in his garage, but in the early 1950s he went to work as a maintenance engineer for Telecon Metals, a firm with open and vacuum furnaces and hot and cold rolling mills. This was at a large factory estate in Crawley (one of the new towns developed to take the overflow from London). He took voluntary redundancy in 1983 after 28 years working for the same firm.

In 1984, over 40 years after he was wounded, Herbert had to have yet another operation as a result of his wounds. His family is doing well. Judith, his daughter, and her husband Frank live nearby at Horsham. They have three children, Shane, Julie, and Michael who have, between them, three sons and two daughters who also live in Horsham.

His son Geoffrey and daughter-in-law Janet live in Willand a village near Tiverton, Devon, a delightful area. They have two daughters, Clare and Lynne. Clare and her husband Shane live close to Geoffrey and have two baby girls, Emily and Laura. Lynne was recently married to Paul and they live in Tiverton.

Herbert considers himself lucky that he survived the war. He still lives at Rusper with his beloved Joyce, and though not in the best of health enjoys his retirement and gets great pleasure when visited by and visiting his children and their families.

Armoured Warfare (2)
George English

George was born in Walberswick in 1919. He left school at 13 and after serving his apprenticeship with Ted Thompson[1] became a bricklayer. He left Walberswick in 1939 to work at his trade in Lincoln and enlisted in August of that year. He intended to join the Royal Navy in order to continue in the seafaring tradition of the English family but:

> Because I was over six feet tall I was persuaded to join the Guards and did six months training as a recruit Guardsman at the Depot in Caterham followed by field training at Pirbright. On completion of my training I joined the 1st Battalion Coldstream Guards who were being mobilised to go to France with the British Expeditionary Force (BEF). However I was detailed to remain in England and go on a signallers course. I rejoined the Battalion when they returned from France after Dunkirk and, under General Montgomery, did infantry training. The

---

[1] There were two builders in Walberswick at that time, Henry Block and Ted Thompson who is best known for the houses he built down 'The Lea', known by the locals as 'Thompson Town'.

Guards Brigade was then converted into an Armoured Division and I became a radio operator/gunner/mechanic in a tank. This training was in preparation for the Second Front invasion of Europe and was carried out in the West Country and Salisbury Plain and later in Yorkshire and Norfolk. When training was completed the Battalion, equipped with Sherman tanks having 75mm guns, was moved to Brighton to await the D-Day landings.

Before that, however, in 1942, I met my wife-to-be Doris (Labad) and we were married in 1943 at Holy Trinity Church, Tottenham, where she lived with her parents. Because of travelling difficulties and the intense bombing in London the only member of my family to attend our wedding was my youngest brother, Tony.

Coldstream Guardsman George English.
(Photo from George English)

Three weeks after the invasion started, George's battalion left England in LCTs (Landing Craft Tanks), landing on the beaches at Arromanches on 1 July and advanced towards Caen. According to the invasion plans Caen was to have been taken on D-Day, but tanks from the German 21st Panzer Division blocked the way. So, on 7 July, General Montgomery, commanding the Allied Land Forces in Normandy, called for an extensive air attack before making a final attempt to capture Caen (Operation CHARNWOOD) by a frontal assault on the 8th. Also that day, HMS *Rodney* bombarded the town with sixteen-inch shells. The combination of bombing and shelling reduced the town to nothing more than rubble. It took two days of heavy fighting with casualties mounting on both sides before, on 10 July, the town was finally taken. Then, on the 17th, under Operation GOODWOOD, followed the battle of the Falaise pocket in which the

Guards Battalion took part. Early in the attack, on 4 August, George's tank was hit by an 88mm armour-piercing shell. The gunner and tank commander were both killed and George, who considered himself lucky, was badly wounded receiving shrapnel wounds down his left side. He was taken to a Field Hospital for treatment and then on to a hospital ship, HMHS *Amsterdam,* to return to England.

However fate hadn't finished with George yet. Halfway across the Channel the ship was torpedoed and many lives were lost including all the nurses. Again luck intervened and a Motor Torpedo Boat (MTB) returning to England rescued him and he was eventually transferred to a hospital in Scotland (supposedly the nearest available place to home). He was given a week's leave and then sent to the Royal Herbert Military Hospital in Woolwich to have the shrapnel removed from his shoulder. He spent some time convalescing at Tonbridge, Kent where, to his disgust as a Guardsman, he had to wear Hospital Blues. (This was a not very smart uniform consisting of an ill-fitting mid-blue serge jacket and trousers, a white shirt, and bright red tie.)

Outside Holy Trinity Church, Tottenham, 1943. (Photo from Doris English)

After his convalescence George returned to the training battalion and had just been detailed to go to Germany as part of a replacement tank crew when peace was declared and he was sent to Norway to mop up the German forces there. He was only there a few weeks when they flew him back to England on a Class B release. Being a bricklayer by trade, he had been released to help in the rebuilding of London.

He went to Aldershot to be demobbed and was placed on the Reserve list for the next six years. This concludes George's wartime story, but Doris's tale and their immediate post-war story continues below.

THE ARMY

Doris English, née Labad

Born in 1920, Doris was among the first women to register for National Service. However, being a Ledger Clerk and working for the Ocean Accident and Guarantee Corporation in Moorgate, London, her job was considered a Reserved Occupation. This was a great disappointment to Doris, as she would rather have joined one of the Armed Services. The girls in the Forces were having a much better time, entertainment-wise anyway.

> Because we had all the records of the company, our department was evacuated when war broke out to houses north, south, and west of London. Apparently nobody expected the war to last as long as it did, so when the leases on the houses ran out in 1942 we had to return to London. We worked on the fifth floor of our building but when the air raid siren sounded we would carry on working, only taking cover when danger from bombs was imminent.

Doris, Rosemary, Janet, and George on Walberswick common.
(Photo from Doris English)

I continued to work there after I was married until George's mother pleaded with me to go to Walberswick where it was safer. From what I remember I think I must have come to Walberswick at the end of July 1944, but when George came back from France, wounded, and was sent to London for his operation I went back too.

As mentioned in George's account (below) we came to Walberswick with our two girls, Rosemary and Janet, in November 1946 and spent a happy ten years there.

*George having fun with the girls.
(Photo from Doris English)*

The move to New Zealand

George:

> We had a couple of rooms with my in-laws in Tottenham, London and by then we had a second child, Janet, so things were a bit crowded. I was working, first, on different building sites, and then at the Tottenham Gas Works on the retorts.

THE ARMY

> We were lucky enough to be allocated one of the Swedish prefabs in Church Lane, Walberswick, and arrived at No. 14 in November 1946 with our two daughters.
>
> Work in the building industry wasn't all that plentiful and with a young family it was a bit of a struggle when we were laid off in the winter months. I decided to go Retort Setting again, working in gas works all over the country. This meant more money, but being away from home wasn't the best and the girls were growing up without me. When we saw an advertisement in the paper that bricklayers were being required in New Zealand we decided to apply and were accepted as New Zealand Immigrants with a free passage to New Zealand. We left England on June 29th 1957 on the SS *Captain Cook* and arrived in New Zealand on August 8th.
>
> We will always remember Denis and Victor Fairs who were at Darsham Station wishing us goodbye as we began our journey to New Zealand. We also still have the Good Luck telegram Mollie and Arthur Sharman sent that was waiting for us on the SS *Captain Cook* when we arrived in Glasgow.

Doris:

> The journey to New Zealand was quite an experience. I was seasick all the time and vowed whatever it was like I would never face the journey home again. [Any one who has suffered from *mal de mer* will sympathise with her.]
>
> We spent the first few weeks with the friends who had sponsored us. But what a shock it was to see the black sand and wild coast after leaving behind the beautiful beach at Walberswick. Of course we were homesick at first but everyone was so kind and friendly that it didn't take us long to adopt the Kiwi way of life.

This finishes the wartime and immediate post-war story of George and Doris. However, the story of the family's life in New Zealand is of such interest to local people that it has been included as an appendix.

THE MOVE TO NEW ZEALAND

George on the sheep farm. (Photo from Doris English)

Janet on the sheep station farm. (Photo from Doris English)

Appendix
George and Doris English and family in New Zealand

Doris writes:

> To begin with George worked as a bricklayer in the local freezing works. Then we answered an advert for a farm labourer. (We could only take a job where a house was provided.) We went out on a farm over 50 miles from civilisation, a sheep station running about 12,000 sheep.
>
> The girls went to school on horseback and George, too, had to learn to ride a horse. When Rosemary was ready for high school we felt we should move closer to a town (over here all children automatically go to high school by the time they are 13). George managed to get a job on the railway here in Eltham as a traffic controller and we lived in a railway house. The schools for both children were close at hand. Once we were able to rent a house George went back to bricklaying and started up his own business and never looked back.
>
> After about a year we managed to buy a ¼ acre section for £75 and later bought the adjacent section for £50 and that's where we built our house. Today a section here would cost from $11,000 upwards (approximately £4,400.) We had to borrow the money from the Public

The house that George built in New Zealand.
(Photo from Doris English)

THE MOVE TO NEW ZEALAND

Trust to build the house, £2,500, and had it all paid off plus interest in 20 years.

I worked as a bacteriologist at the New Zealand Rennet Co. for 18 years, which helped to fill the coffers. I knew nothing about it when I started – didn't even know what rennet was – but I loved the work in the laboratory.

The girls were teenagers in the era of early marriages and both got married when they were young. At the time we felt they were tying themselves down to family responsibilities before they had had much experience of life. But it was meant to be as, unfortunately, they both lost their husbands in their early 40s; but they had had at least 25 years together. Rosemary's husband died of cancer and Janet's husband was stung on his neck by a wasp and was dead within half an hour. It was a terrible shock.

My elder daughter Rosemary was married to Roger and they had three children, Vicky, Colin, and Karen.

Vicky was always interested in Rugby, like her dad, and always wanted to play. She started Women's Rugby in Taranaki and then went on to New Zealand Women's Rugby. She became trainer and coach for the New Zealand Women's Team, then selector and finally their manager. She went over to Holland last year (1998) to win the World Cup for New Zealand. She is married to Jeff and has two boys: Jamie who is 14 and Anthony 12.

Colin has been in the Navy since he was 17. He began, as a Wine Steward but is now a Petty Officer. He has

Rosemary on the farm in New Zealand. (Photo from Doris English)

done lots of overseas trips and has virtually been all around the world. He got married a year or so ago.

Karen is a bit of a rebel but is improving with age. She has two children though the chap she has married isn't their father. They work on a small farm. Her boys are Jesse, aged 5 and Dylan 4.

My younger daughter Janet was married to Lyle and they had four children: Jackie, Sandra, and twin boys Dallas and Glenn.

Jackie's partner is Chappie and they have two boys, Zane 11 and Jordan 7. Jackie works at the High School with problem students. She is studying for an Education Degree.

Sandra is married to James and they have a little girl Ashleigh who is six and our only great granddaughter. Unfortunately Sandra has suffered from eczema and asthma ever since she was a baby, so life is difficult for her. She has received her diploma as a Caregiver.

Dallas has been in England for over five years now. Last year Janet and Jackie went over to England to visit him in London. They all went to stay with my sister in Leiston and went to Walberswick from there. Jackie and Dallas were very impressed with the Suffolk scenery.

Glenn, the other twin, is engaged to be married and has a good job in the dairy industry. He came over to England to visit Dallas about four years ago and did a tour of Europe as well.

As we have seven grandchildren and seven great-grandchildren, we feel we have done our bit to increase the population of New Zealand!

Both Rosemary and Janet have now got new partners. We are happy for them, as they were far too young to spend the rest of their lives alone.

When we arrived here it was certainly a land of 'milk and honey', but as in the rest of the world times have changed. But it is still a good place to be and we have never regretted taking the plunge.

A gunner, policeman, and fireman
George Rimmington Rogers

George Rimmington Rogers was born at Walberswick on 9 April 1917 and was the only son of George Rimmington Rogers senior who, apart from handing on his name to his son, also passed on to him the garage and lock-up on the village green in Walberswick.

To put things in a proper chronological order: George, at age 17, volunteered and joined the Royal Artillery on 17 November 1934, for a three-year stretch. Number 840129 Gunner G. R. Rogers did his initial training at the Depot Woolwich. Those were the days before the British Army had been mechanised and the accompanying picture shows him in breeches, putties, and spurs with a white lanyard on his right shoulder and carrying a walking out crop. Having successfully completed his training he was then posted to an Artillery Brigade at Aldershot (this was before the name Regiment was used other than when referring to the whole of the Royal Regiment of Artillery). He was then posted to Deepcut for further training in preparation for the Royal Artillery to be mechanised. Not long afterwards he was posted to Gibraltar and while he was there met up with a Major Powell (retired) who lived, at that time, at Bracken Cottage on the common at Walberswick. Major Powell who was a keen yachtsman had sailed there from Walberswick and he promptly invited George to have dinner on board the yacht.

George in full uniform with walking out crop
(Photo from Dulcie Rogers)

In 1935, at the time when Mussolini invaded Ethiopia, he was posted to Palestine. Whilst there he bought a prayer book and would collect flowers from the Garden of Gethsemane and place it in the pages of the book.

Having served his agreed three years with the colours George was discharged and put on the Army Reserve for 9 years.

He then joined the Essex Police and was stationed at Chelmsford. He was there when war broke out and, although in the Army Reserve, his occupation

THE ARMY

*With fellow recruits and instructors at Woolwich. George is seated 2nd from left. The gun on the right is probably an 18 pdr.
(Photo from Dulcie Rogers)*

*George, when in the police at Chelmsford, row 2, 2nd from right.
(Photo from Dulcie Rogers)*

A GUNNER, POLICEMAN, AND FIREMAN

*George, on left, with crew of self-propelled gun.
(Photo from Dulcie Rogers)*

*George with the Belgian family who became life-long friends.
(Photo from Dulcie Rogers)*

THE ARMY

in the police force placed him on the reserved occupation list. He was not happy about that, but it was not until 1942 he was able to rejoin the Royal Artillery where he was posted to the 42nd Anti-Tank Regiment. It was not long before his Regiment was sent to North Africa to join the 8th Army; subsequently they took part in the Anzio landings and George went through the whole of the Italian campaign.

The regiment then moved to Belgium and George was there when peace in Europe was declared. He returned to England and was finally demobbed in 1946.

George was not happy unless he was in uniform and doing something for the public good, so in March 1947 he joined the London Fire Brigade.

His station was called out to attend fires or other emergencies two or three times a week and on a number of occasions he became wet to the skin and unable to dry himself off for many hours. On one occasion in April 1947 he was working in the flooded fenland in Norfolk, pumping water for a couple of days and got soaked; in this case it was over two days before he returned to his station and was able to change into dry clothes.

*George, 2nd from right, middle row, as a member of the London Fire Brigade crew.
(Photo from Dulcie Rogers)*

In January 1948 he attended a fire at Welwyn Council Offices and was the driver of the fire engine. When another fireman mistakenly took George's jacket, he proceeded to drive in his shirt sleeves in spite of the bitter weather. He suffered severely from the intense cold and was never well again, becoming crippled with rheumatoid arthritis. In May 1949 he was discharged from the London Fire Brigade as unfit for service.

George Rimmington Rogers was one of a rare breed of men who put duty and the welfare of others before himself. His health continued to deteriorate and he died at the comparatively young age of 67 on 15 August 1984.

George had a daughter Ellen. After George died his wife Dulcie left Walberswick. She now lives in Gunton, Lowestoft, not far from Ellen who keeps in close touch with her.

Memories of Home and the Far East
Charles J. Harwood

Charles Harwood was born at Bootle, Lancashire and came to live in Walberswick after the war, having met a Walberswick girl, Margo Fairs, when he was posted to Blythburgh in 1940. He enlisted at Crosby, Merseyside, in the 66th Anti Tank Regiment (TA) in August 1939. Half of the strength of the Regiment was made up of ex-pupils from the Merseyside Merchant Taylors School. His initial training was done at Burton Manor and Rugeley, Staffordshire:

> When we were there we prepared the Regiment for active service and were issued with our rifles and 5 rounds of ammunition and told: 'Keep your rifle with you at all times and use your ammunition sparingly', which I thought was rather comical.
>
> Just after the fall of France in June 1940 our Regiment, with its two-pounder guns, was hastily sent to defend the East Coast. I was part of the rearguard and went by rail after the main body of the unit had left Crosby. We went to Halesworth and were met at the station by our transport and taken to Blythburgh.
>
> At Blythburgh we set up camp by a barn on Toby's Walks not far from the A12. We also had a few tents pitched on the grass verges nearby. My job, with others, was to man the concrete pillbox on the corner of the Blythburgh to Walberswick road and I remember the kindness of Mrs Chester King, who lived on the opposite side of the road, keeping

THE ARMY

*Early days. The Bulldog Breed. Charles, front row, 2nd left.
(Photo from Charles Harwood)*

the guard supplied with hot cocoa. This was very acceptable, especially when the weather was cold.

We built another defence position about 40 to 50 yards from the pillbox up Toby's Walks. This position was made up from railway lines taken from the old narrow gauge Southwold to Halesworth railway at Blythburgh, and from iron corrugated sheeting from the unused Wenhaston Station. Our maintenance and repair centre for the vehicles and guns was set up at the rear of the White Hart Inn where the mechanics and artificers worked.

It was while I was stationed at Blythburgh that I met Margo Fairs, who was to become my wife. It happened on Friday, 8th August 1940. The day was very hot and we had been working late to complete another vantage point. After tea my pal, Bob Corten, wanted me to go to a dance that evening being held in Blythburgh Village Hall. I was tired out and really didn't want to go but eventually he persuaded me. When we got into the hall I was introduced to Margo who was a nurse on leave from the Norfolk and Norwich Hospital. I found her most attractive and this perked me up so after the dance I asked her if I could

MEMORIES OF HOME AND THE FAR EAST

escort her home and she agreed. Margo lived in Walberswick and as we were not allowed to leave Blythburgh I walked her as far as I could down the Mile Field road. Eight months later we were married in Walberswick church.

I stayed in Blythburgh for about six months and then we were moved to the Drill Hall at Halesworth for a short time and then the whole Regiment moved to Deddington, Oxfordshire, where we underwent training to improve our handling of the guns and increase our physical fitness. It was while we were there that the BBC paid us a visit. Six of our wagons had to go round in circles while they photographed us – I think this was just for propaganda purposes. Following that we were sent to Alfriston on the Sussex Downs, not too far from Beachy Head, to meet the increasing threat of invasion.

Our next move was to Hull (Birstwick) until August 1942 when I was transferred to the 321 Anti-Tank Regiment (The Gordon Highlanders) and posted to Beeston near Wroxham. The Gordon Highlanders had recently converted from machine guns to six-pounder anti-tank guns. There were four of us who had been posted from Blythburgh and the Sergeant-Major said a funny thing. He asked us: 'Do you know why you've been brought here?' and I said: 'Yes'. He said: 'Why?' I replied, just as a joke, 'It's because of the morale of your Scottish troops.' He didn't take much to me after that. In fact we were posted there to make up their numbers and help them get used to the guns and assist them in their gunnery training.

Shortly after that we were posted to India. We sailed from Greenock on the SS *Stratheden* and I was put in charge of issuing the food. What I had to do was to go down into the galley and make sure that each Regiment had enough bread, which was baked daily on board, and take all the food out in one go to the mess-deck.

We disembarked at Bombay and went by train to a place called Ahmadnagar and then on to Burma. Our Battery, the 321/122, flew over 'The Hump',[2] and we landed at an airstrip that had been bulldozed

---

[2] In 1942 the Japanese had cut the Burma Road and so the troops in China could no longer be supplied overland. The only way supplies could be got to our troops in Burma and China was by air flying over the mountainous terrain on the flank of the Himalayas. Pilots referred to this as 'flying over the Hump'.

out of jungle country not far from Myitkyina, the start of the railway there that runs south to Mandalay. [See map, p. 76.]

This railway was used to supply the army in Burma; it was the 36th Indian Division and they helped in the shipment of food ammunition, petrol, and other supplies to the Chinese and Allied Armies in Burma.

We advanced south until we came to Myitkyina where we found that some of the railway lines and equipment had been damaged. The engineers came and tried to fix the rolling stock. There were no engines to haul these but somebody, somehow or another found out that if you took the tyres off the wheels of a Jeep they would fit exactly on the railway line; the gauge was the same. We put the Jeeps onto the railway and one of them would haul a couple of wagons. Eventually when we advanced further on and got down towards Mandalay we had a railway service going backwards and forwards.

Charles in India.
(Photo from Charles Harwood)

When we got to Mogaung, the day before Christmas, I went to Supplies and was given a live pig and six chickens for Christmas dinner. One of the men had worked in an abattoir in Aberdeen so we were lucky because he knew how to deal with the live pig. He knew where to hit it on the head and used a sledgehammer to kill it and then he dressed it. Our Christmas dinner was a great success and the pig tasted lovely – a lot better than the hard tack we'd been having.

One day we'd been having quite a tussle with the Japs and it was always our policy, about an hour before dark, to consolidate our

The railway jeep, substituting for engines on the lines at Myitkyina.

(Photo from Charles Harwood)

position. So this particular day, as I have said, there had been quite a battle going on and we got to this weir where some trees had been knocked down. Now we started to settle down for the night along this ridge and make this our point of resistance in case of attack. Anyway it was a couple of days after this and I was acting Quartermaster at the time. We got orders to advance so we went round and gave everybody a tot of rum. The officer, Lieut. Harman, was sitting on one of these tree trunks with Sergeant Major Webster. I said to the officer, 'There's some left, you may as well use it up', and as I walked away the Sergeant Major shouted, 'Any more for rum?' and there was a sudden dash for it – naturally. Just at that precise moment a Japanese shell came over and hit the tree trunk they were sitting on. There were 23 killed and 40 odd injured. The officer was a very good friend of mine. I know I said at the time to one of the chaps: 'It was all my fault. I shouldn't have shouted about the rum.' They all said: 'Oh, take that out

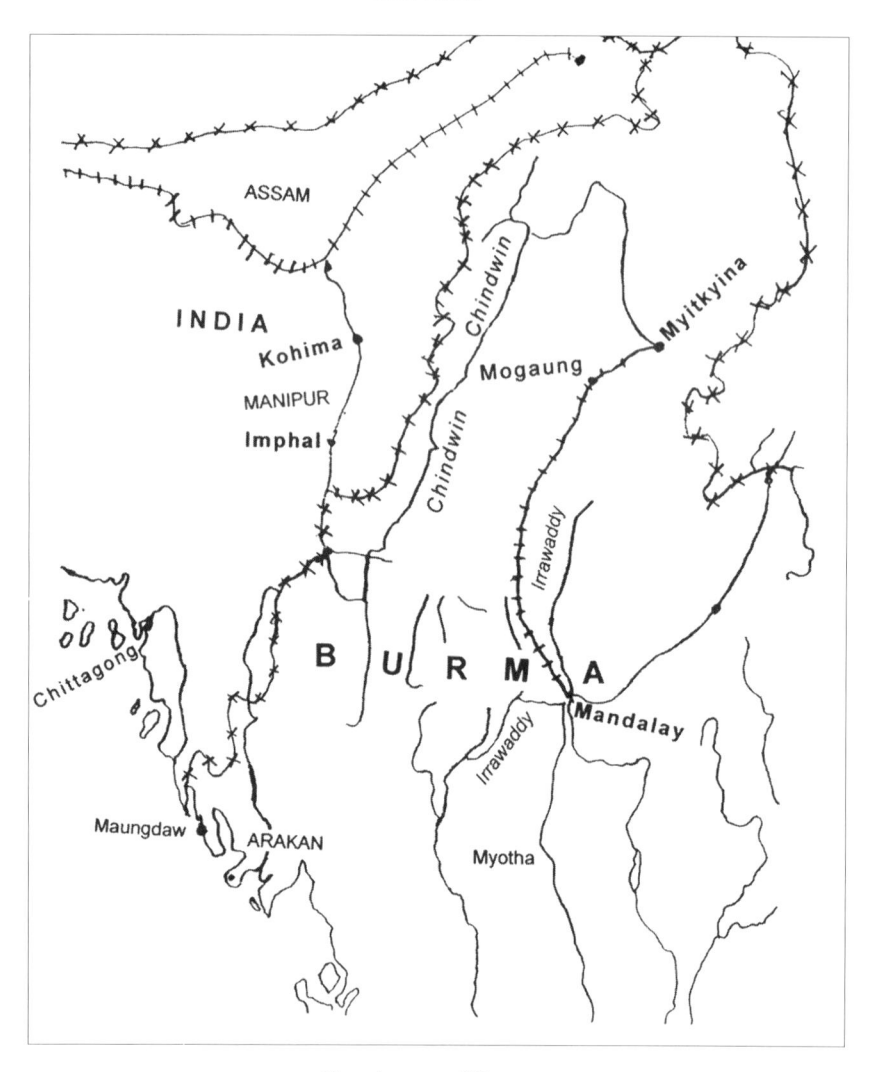

Sketch map of Burma

of your mind, don't worry about that. It's not your fault.' But I still blame myself and will never forget it.

We broke out from there and kept advancing south to a place called Hopin. We stayed there for a wee while. This place had been used as a pleasure centre for the Japanese Army and we came across a lot of huts there. After taking safety precautions, in case they were booby-trapped, we broke into one of them. Well. I have never seen so many contraceptives in all my life, there were thousands of them. That's all there was in this hut, they were kept there for the Japanese welfare home. The Japanese army used to have geisha girls and they would go with the camp. Whenever we came across them we captured them – well, we had to. One particular chick was very, very nasty and she spat at me. We put her in a tent by herself. Most of the Japs we came across were smallish but she was quite well built and tall; the other geisha girls, though, seemed to be about the same size as the average Japanese soldier.

At one point we were at the same place for twelve days and lost a number of men from Japanese snipers. We were very short of water, especially for the wounded and they asked for volunteers to look for water. I volunteered and we found some. It was just a trickle and we had to dig a hole to allow enough water to accumulate for us to be able to scoop it out. We had mules with us and after filling the mule panniers with water we started back to the camp. We were about 50 yards from the camp when the Japanese snipers opened fire on us, trying to smash a hole in the water panniers.

Anyway, we arrived back at camp and, having got some water, I made a cup of tea and asked one of the infantrymen passing by if he would like a sup. He eagerly accepted and had a couple of sups saying it was the best cup he'd ever had. He put the cup down and was just going on his way when a sniper shot him dead. I felt terrible about that.

Well, we kept advancing down south and next came to a river, which we had to cross. There was a small island in the middle of this river occupied by a troop of Japanese who had a mortar. This mortar was one that was strapped to the knee and could be fired from there. They were shelling us with this and they held us up for two or three days before they finally retreated. We thought afterwards there would probably have been about fifteen of them.

It was about this time when we were about 250 yards from the Japanese when a Staff Officer came along and told us that Lady Mountbatten wanted to see and talk to the front line troops. He pointed to us and told her that we were the front line troops. Just as she was talking to our lads a burst of gun fire came from the real front line troops, Lady Mountbatten looked at the Staff Officer and gave him a real ticking off for misleading her. His face went as red as the tabs on his uniform.

The Engineers threw a bridge over the river for us and we continued to a place south of Myotha when we were brought to a halt. After a couple of days we were told the war was over in Burma. We were sent from there to Chittagong and Poona, and on to a place about four miles outside and started training there for the invasion of Singapore when the war was declared over. We were moved then from Poona to Bombay and flew on to Karachi ready to be sent back to the UK but, while we were waiting there, they started letting our people who had been Japanese prisoners of war through and they were given precedence so we were held back. Eventually we were flown via Durban to Heliopolis and it was there that I bought a huge basket of fruit to take home. We finally landed at Brize Norton and from there went to Chelsea Barracks, London.

When I got to Chelsea Barracks I was told to report to the officer in charge. I went in and there was Captain Birfield, the same chap who had been in charge of the depot in Burma where we got all our supplies. I was supposed to stay there and catch the London to Manchester midnight train but he said, 'We have a good canteen here, you go and have a meal'. I had just got the meal on the table when the Sergeant came dashing in calling for me: 'Quick. Come on, come on', he said, 'we've rushed things through a bit for you. Go to the wagon outside, the driver will get you to the station. Here's a permit for your travel. You'll be met at Manchester station and taken to the demob centre.' So instead of leaving at midnight I left about two o'clock in the afternoon. When I got to the demob centre I was the only one there. The staff there was waiting for a big shipment in from Liverpool so everybody was saying: 'Try this on. Try that on.' But I was anxious to get home.

I still had this huge basket of fruit that I had carted with me everywhere and eventually we got to Lime Street station. I thought, oh, I can't be bothered with a bus, so I caught a taxi home. I knocked on the door and when they saw me this was the first time the family knew I was even in the country. It was a bit of a shock for them, especially for Margo. We'd been apart for so long that it was like our marriage starting all over again.

> After the war I came to live in Walberswick and worked at my trade as a bricklayer. I have always loved football and with others formed a Walberswick football team with Margo as the Secretary. My position in the team was goalkeeper. In the five seasons before I left Walberswick the team won at least one trophy each season.
>
> My family and I visit Walberswick as often as possible. I look around now and see a greatly changed village. It does not seem to have the characters I remember when we lived there immediately after the war. Characters like Ted Thompson, a local builder, Harold Piper, husband of the local school teacher, George Rogers who owned a garage by the village green, Arthur Sharman senior who was the parade marshal for the British Legion Armistice Day church parades and, of course, 'Ginger' (Ernest) Winyard, the ever cheerful publican of the Anchor Inn. Happy memories.

Charles returned to Crosby in 1946 and worked at Costain's, a well-known civil engineering firm, until 1982 when he retired. In 1999 as the result of diabetes he had to have his left leg amputated but he handles this setback with the same courage and determination that carried him through his time in the war and will not give in. As he says: 'you have got to make the best of life and I am lucky to have returned safely from the war. I have a wonderful wife and a close-knit loving family for which I am thankful.'

Home Guard to National Service Gunner
Derek Kett

Derek Kett was born in Blythburgh in 1929, so was only 10 years old when war broke out. He went to Blythburgh and Reydon Schools and joined the Army Cadets at Wenhaston at the age of nearly 14. When he was old enough he joined the Home Guard and was employed as a messenger, using his own bicycle. He relates:

> The Home Guard would use the church tower as a lookout and one evening I was given a message to deliver to the police station about ¾ of a mile away, at the bottom of the hill on the main London road. I left my bicycle on the side of the road and dashed up the hill to deliver the message. When I returned, there waiting for me, in the form of the

THE ARMY

Law, was Inspector Bird from Halesworth who told me I would be charged with leaving a 'vehicle' unattended, which could have been of use to the enemy.

Poor Derek. This was the time when we expected the Germans to invade us and Derek really thought he would be summoned to appear before the court. However when Inspector Bird saw he had nearly frightened the life out of the lad he relented and was satisfied with giving him a severe ticking off, telling him never to leave his bicycle unattended again – he never did.

Derek in front of a Sherman-mounted self-propelled 25 pdr in the Canal Zone. (Photo from Derek Kett)

Derek remembers the many times when British and American aircraft crashed around the area, especially the time when the Kennedy plane exploded and the pieces fell over Blythburgh Fen (see pp. 240–1 of *Suffolk Memories*). During air raids everyone would look for pieces of shrapnel to keep as souvenirs, and Derek remembers one particular time when he picked up a piece which could only have just fallen because he found it was too hot to hold.

Derek left school at age 14 and went to work at the Dickon Nurseries, Walberswick and, although he was in the Home Guard, would dearly have

*On checkpoint duty at Fayid in the Canal Zone.
(Photo from Derek Kett)*

THE ARMY

liked to join one of the Services. Of course he was too young and was working in horticulture, which was a reserved occupation. The war was over but people were still being called up so Derek decided he would try to get a berth at Lowestoft and go fishing. He went for an interview and was accepted and expected to sail the following Sunday, but he got a message from the Labour Exchange in Southwold telling him he couldn't leave his job at the nurseries. Nothing daunted, he next tried to get into the Palestine Police but still to no avail. By this time there was a demand for Bevan Boys who would be called up and sent to work in the coal mines instead of one of the Services. Derek had no intention of become a miner working down the pits so he tried to enlist in the Army. This time, to his delight, he was successful and joined the Royal Regiment of Artillery. He did his basic training in the Royal Artillery training depot at Oswestry in Shropshire following which he was posted to Rhyl in Wales for vehicle driver training and from there to Bovingdon for Armoured Fighting Vehicle (AFV) driver training in the use of self-propelled guns. Having successfully passed this he was posted to a holding unit at Woolwich barracks. Derek relates:

This was just before Queen Elizabeth's Coronation in 1953 and the barracks were full of police who were being prepared to take part in the Coronation. All the regular barrack accommodation had been taken over by them. We were therefore given empty palliasses and bedded down in a broken-down open stable for three days until we enplaned (the straw for the palliasses never did arrive), to join 'V' Battery, 6th Field Regiment Royal Artillery, which had self-propelled 25pdr guns, in the Canal Zone in Egypt.

Brewing up whilst on a Scheme in the Canal Zone. (Photo from Derek Kett)

82

HOME GUARD TO NATIONAL SERVICE GUNNER

One of the tasks we had to do in the Canal Zone was to man roadblocks. Vehicles were stopped, people checked, and the vehicles searched for illegal arms, ammunition, and explosives [see picture on p. 81 above]. One day a car came roaring up and tried to break through the barrier without being checked. I had been trained in the use of the Bren machine gun and considered myself an expert shot, so when the vehicle came swerving round the chicane I brought up my Bren gun ready to fire at the vehicle. I was most peeved, however, when the soldier who was actually stopping the vehicles sharply brought his Sten gun up and with two rapid shots burst the two near-side tyres. The driver of the vehicle lost control and it somersaulted down a sandy bank. The occupants, badly shaken, were arrested. It was lucky that in the furore nobody was killed.

After 12 months in the Canal Zone the Regiment returned to England and we were then posted to Hohne Barracks in Germany training for

Derek (unseen) driving a Sexton self-propelled 25 pdr on to a low loader. (Photo from Derek Kett)

the defence of Germany in case of attack, including nuclear, from the Russians.

After about a year I had completed my two years National Service and returned to Woolwich and thence to civilian life. I had served for two happy and interesting years in the army and I am now content and proud at having done service for my country'.

In the Auxiliary Territorial Service (ATS)
Renée Dowse née Kett

Renée Kett was born and bred in Blythburgh and went to Blythburgh and Reydon Area School where she was at one time the Girls' School Captain. She left school and home at the age of 14 and went to work as a nanny in London with a Harley Street doctor who lived in Kensington. She stayed with them until the early part of 1939, then found herself a job at Selfridges and was there when the war broke out in September of that year. Renée writes:

> I went back to Blythburgh when Don, my brother, returned home wounded from the Dieppe raid and my mother could no longer stand the strain of looking after him. During that time I met my husband to be, Ted Dowse, who was in the Army and stationed at Aldeburgh, but before we had time to marry I was called up into the ATS.
>
> I was stationed at the Talavera Camps, Northampton, where I did my early 'square bashing'. This was the same camp and same time that the Queen, as Princess Elizabeth, was doing her training; she went on to become a driver whereas I was sent to train as one of the G.L. girls, better known as Radio Location girls. Here I did so much study and had to learn about geometry and trigonometry plus basic electrical 'bumph' – things unheard of at that time, especially for girls. At the end of it all we were given a course in aircraft recognition.
>
> Having completed this training I was posted to the 599th Heavy AA Battery, Royal Artillery. Our task was to pick up the signals from incoming enemy aircraft and plot them to the guns. We often had to sleep under the gun installations when on duty call.

IN THE AUXILIARY TERRITORIAL SERVICE (ATS)

We also had to learn how to lay roads using stones and rocks to make a flat surface. I remember one particular February day when it was bitterly cold having to help lay a flat road so our AA Battery equipment could be moved onto the site.

We normally slept in a tin Nissen hut with a wood-burner stove in the centre. Our mattresses came in three sections that were known as 'biscuits' (most uncomfortable) and these would have to be piled at the end of the bed with the blankets and sheets neatly assembled on top for room inspection each morning. Woe betide anyone who did not get a perfectly aligned result.

Renée (on the right) outside one of the Radio Location girls' huts. (Photo from Renée Dowse)

As well as normal duties with the guns we would also be given cook house duties, involving scrubbing cooking pots and pans and peeling hundreds of potatoes using cold water – ugh. My biggest nightmare was how to get my thick hair cut to exactly 3ins off my collar under my peaked cap. On parade every morning the officer in charge would come along and to inspect us and some officers would actually measure the gap between my collar and the cap. As I have a short neck this was difficult and I was often given extra cook house duties because the gap wasn't correct.

It was not always 'doom and gloom', though. We did have some fun times when off duty. During these times we kept to our own groups – Radio Location girls didn't mingle with the cooks or drivers and we went on our own outings. This also applied to the Nissen huts – Radio Location girls had their own huts in one group. Sometimes we went on route marches and had some pretty tough sergeants to train us in drill

THE ARMY

and marching. Our group had one tough Royal Marine Sergeant who delighted in yelling and swearing at us girls – we were very fit in those days and took it all in our stride.

Our Battery was moved near Coventry to a gun site defending that city. This was at the time of the blitz and the bombing was very heavy so we were kept very busy. I was then put in charge of teaching some American soldiers how to operate our equipment. I found this task somewhat daunting but I coped with them and the teaching.

Whilst I was on that site we had a direct hit on our camp, causing much havoc. A lot of my friends were killed at that time and I don't like talking about it.

Later on I was sent to Oswestry in Shropshire where I furthered my radio skills. I loved it there. The local people were so good to us, inviting us into their homes.

My fiancé Ted Dowse was also in the army. He was in the infantry, the Hampshire Regiment, and stationed at Aldershot so we didn't see much of each other. By 1943, though, everybody knew that something big was in the air. Training was intensifying for the invasion of Europe, and as we knew that he would be going overseas we decided to get married. We applied for leave and were married in Holy Trinity Church, Blythburgh, on 15 September 1943 and after a short honeymoon we both had to return to our respective units.

June 6th 1944 was a dreadful day for me. As I sat under the big guns in the Command Room, I heard all the aircraft flying overhead to Normandy knowing that my husband Ted was somewhere amongst all this movement of troops. I heard much later that he had sailed from Portsmouth on one of the Landing Craft and landed near Le Hamel on the beach close to Arromanches, Normandy, on 22 June 1944 with the 7th Battalion Hampshire Regiment (later the Royal Hampshire Regiment), 130 Brigade, 43rd Wessex Division.

It was many months before I saw him again. Meanwhile I was kept busy around the industrial areas of North England until I was finally discharged in 1945. I later moved to Southwold.

Nine years later, employment being difficult, we decided to emigrate and on 2 September 1954 sailed from Southampton on the Orient liner

IN THE AUXILIARY TERRITORIAL SERVICE (ATS)

SS *Otranto* arriving at Sydney in Australia on 13 October. We never regretted moving 'down under' and have enjoyed a good life here.

Ted returned to Normandy with other ex-Servicemen for the 50th Anniversary of the D-Day landings in 1994. He was given the Memorial Medal with a certificate signed by François Mitterand.

I still write regularly to my surviving brother Derek at Blythburgh, sister Poppy at Reydon, and sister Ruby who lives in South Africa. I also keep up a correspondence with a Mr Docwra who used to have the Red Lion in Southwold and a Mrs Wurr, my English teacher of childhood days at the Area School at Reydon. Mr Docwra was once the Boys' School Captain at Reydon though not when I was Girls' School Captain.

On 28 February 1998 at age 77 my dear Ted passed away and I miss him dreadfully, but my three sons, Graeme, John, and Richard are a great comfort to me.

I will always love Southwold, Blythburgh, and Walberswick, which have many happy memories for me, but I am quite content to end my days here in Kanahooka, New South Wales, Australia.

The SS Otranto *in which Renée sailed with Ted to Australia.*
(Photo from Dulcie Rogers)

THE ARMY

BEF to Burma
George Turner Stanyer

George Stanyer (1913–1997) owned a cottage for over twenty years in the lane known as Daisy Bank, just below the magnificent Holy Trinity church, Blythburgh. This was used as a second home and he and his family stayed there frequently and would take part in the life of the village.

Apart from his wartime in the Forces, he spent a lifetime of service (45 years) with the famous paper manufacturers, Wiggins Teape, starting in 1931 at age 18 as a clerk in the Head Office and working his way through various departments. He became a Director of Wiggins Teape and Alex Pirie (Sales) in 1961, then finally, in 1965, Marketing Manager Fine Papers.

He joined the Territorial Army in the Royal Regiment of Artillery in 1938 and at the time of the Munich Crisis he was on duty on the roof of Simpsons, Piccadilly with a Lewis anti-aircraft machine gun. War broke out and his Regiment formed part of the British Expeditionary Force that went to France.

George's brother, General John Stanyer, writes:

> On the 9th of June Paris fell to the advancing German Panzer Divisions. George was serving in a Royal Artillery Regiment somewhere east of Paris. The German armies were advancing west, having by-passed Paris. They were moving on towards Cherbourg and Brittany. Churchill agreed with the French President, Reynaud, that a new defensive line should jointly be established in Brittany along the river Loire. George's unit along with many others moved west in support of these proposals. Almost immediately the French Government asked for an armistice, at which point Churchill ordered that all British troops should withdraw from France and measures were taken to provide shipping to achieve this task.
>
> The Cunard troopship *Lancastria* left Liverpool on 14 June and headed for St Nazaire on the Loire. On 17 June the ship had embarked around 5,200 troops and a number of refugees including women and children by about noon. At around 3.45 p.m. a single German bomber hit the ship with a salvo of four bombs, which cut off all communications and started fires fore and aft. George rarely told of the sheer horror facing the hundreds of soldiers below decks who had to get up on deck to survive. (George told James O'Brien, a fellow officer, that he was holding the first cup of hot tea that he had had for some weeks, just as

the ship broke in two in front of him). He jumped into the oily Loire, to be picked up by one of the many French fishing boats that appeared on the scene. The survivors, including George, ultimately reached England in a variety of ships. Over 3,000 men perished in this one tragic incident.

Given the scale of the disaster, Winston Churchill, placed a 'D-notice' on the publication of the news, in the interests of public morale; however the news was published in the *Daily Mail* on 26 July 1940. This was one of the worst disasters in maritime history. [*Defence + notice.* A government notice to news editors not to publish items on specified subjects, for reasons of security.]

Details of the sinking are held in the Cunard Archives of the University of Liverpool.

A happier event occurred in July 1941 when George married his sweetheart, Edna Rose Hyam. He was at that time a 2nd Lieutenant and it was not long before he was sent with his unit, 87th Anti-Tank Battery, to Burma. He served out there for almost four years in SEAC (South East Asia Command), seeing action mostly in the Arakan and Manipur area.

An officer who served with George told of his great sense of humour which helped him and the soldiers he served with whilst fighting in the dreadful conditions that all who served in Burma had to endure.

He had a remarkable rapport with the men under his command and was unquestionably the most popular officer in his unit, probably because he empathised so genuinely with their concerns and feelings, so far from home and in such unpleasant circumstances. Casualties affected him deeply, although he tried not to show his concern too obviously. An example of this was when George was in command of a reconnaissance patrol in the Chin Hills near Tiddim. They were ambushed and the leading scout, a young Welsh boy of about nineteen or twenty years old, just ahead of George on the jungle path, was hit, and withering fire made it impossible even to recover his body. It took George a long time to get over the loss of this young soldier.

One time when he had gone out from his dugout with a patrol and was on his way back he saw small sheets of paper blowing about in the undergrowth. Now George always carried with him, when operating in forward positions in the jungle, letters he had received from his wife Edna and this practice probably saved his life. Seeing these pieces of paper it was clear that the dugout had been discovered and ransacked and there was little doubt that a contingent of Japanese was waiting to give the returning patrol a hot reception. Having been alerted by what they saw, George and his patrol were ready and it was the Japanese who got the hot reception.

He had quite an eventful time whilst in Burma as the following few selected items from 'C' Troop War Diary, 87th Anti Tank Battery RA of 1944 shows. He signed each of these entries:

June 6th: Jap lobbed a few shells over early.

June 15th: More rain. New latrines being dug. Report that 800 Japs are approaching Huigthangong. Some firing heard from the south.

June 17th: Work continued on barbed wire. Rain ceased, for how long?

June 18th: Sikhs opened fire with Bren on something (what?) across the road to south.

June 19th: Believe it or not the 'Sun is shining'. Message sent to sites re Noel Coward's show.
Japs started shelling approx. 16.10 hrs.

June 22nd: Morgan and Jackson on Site 1 attempt to get 15cwt [truck] out of harbour area unsuccessful, mud knee deep. Capt. Stanyer and Bombardier English on recce. Percentage of personnel to go for hot baths tomorrow. Must wear oldest clothes, will be issued with new outfit after bath.

June 25th: Capt. Stanyer to Imphal. Capt. Stanyer returned with food rations (11/2 issue)

July 7th: Balls up on Site 1 ammo. Now find that they are 72 H.E. rounds short. Have we dropped ONE?

July 8th: Fresh check made of all 40 mm ammo. Capt. Stanyer to B.H.Q. with report 09.30 hrs.
Major Greg called, remarked that it was 'not a good morning'.

July 17th: Capt. Stanyer's jeep in head-on collision with jeep of 2i/c 129 Fld. Regt. Just outside T.H.Q. Capt. Stanyer suffered cut on forehead.

The casualty list of the unit George served with in Burma during 1942-45 was as follows: 7 killed in action, 3 died on active service, 19 wounded.

Captain George Turner Stanyer returned to civilian life with Wiggins Teape in November 1945, having served his country well and leaving memories of great comradeship to all with whom he came in contact during his service in the Forces.

Chapter 3
THE ROYAL AIR FORCE

A widow of war

Doris Smith, formerly Fairs née Buck

Mrs Doris Smith's first husband, Flight Sergeant Geoffrey Fairs, RAF, who was born at Manor Farm, Huntingfield, near Halesworth, and brought up in Walberswick, was lost in action in June 1944. *Suffolk Memories* (p. 5) records this fact and gives a short description of him, his marriage, his service in the forces, especially in the Royal Air Force, and what happened to him and his aircraft. It also records his commemoration on the Runnymede Memorial.

His widow, though, would like to tell her story of how she met Geoffrey

A happy family: (from left) Geoffrey and Doris; Harry Moreton who married Audrey Fairs; and Jack Fairs who married Grace Roberts.
(Photo from Doris Smith)

and subsequent events as they affected her. Doris has kept many of the letters he wrote and has in her possession his Royal Canadian Air Force Pilot's Flying Log Book. This contains entries from the time he was a student pilot through to the record of his being 'Certified missing from operations 6/7th June' and then stamped 'Death Presumed'. At Doris's request this has been included in story form, showing how he advanced in his training to become a pilot and his subsequent postings and missions.

We begin with Doris's meeting with Geoffrey and her personal reminiscences:

Flight Sgt Pilot Geoffrey Fairs (Photo from Doris Smith)

> I first met Geoffrey in 1939 when I was shopping at the International Stores, Leiston. Geoffrey was serving behind the counter and we struck up a friendship. It was not long before we fell in love and were walking out together. We would go to the pictures at the Picture House in Leiston or take long walks. After I met Geoffrey's parents we would go to the Barn Cinema at Walberswick, sadly no longer in existence, or go to whist drives in Walberswick and Blythburgh. The Fairs family were all avid card players and Mrs Fairs an expert at the game. It was through attending these whist drives I got to know a lot of people in the two villages.
>
> These happy days did not last very long, however, for in July 1939 Geoffrey was called up with the militia and was sent to the 502 Training Battery, 5th Anti-Aircraft (ack-ack) Militia Depot at Arborfield near Reading and was there for some time. In May 1940 he was posted to the 156 AA Battery, 82nd AA Regiment, which was preparing to join the Norwegian Expeditionary Force and on 10 May 1940 they sailed for Norway.

Geoffrey returned to England on 12 June 1940 travelling in HMS *Devonshire*. King Haakon of Norway was on the same ship and Geoffrey saw him several times during the voyage and was much impressed by the King's height. He was a very tall man.

On 7 June 1940 King Haakon VII of Norway, together with his government, escaped from the German invading force. They embarked on the cruiser HMS *Devonshire* at Tromsö and sailed for London to go into exile in England.

Geoffrey and I didn't see much of each other during those times but we exchanged letters as often as we could and I missed him dreadfully. However, in August 1940 he was posted to Loughton in Essex with the 274th (HAC[1]) AA Battery, 86 (HAC) AA Regiment. Whilst he was there things were much easier and we would meet quite frequently and he would sometimes get leave.

Geoffrey standing beside one of the 'cumbersome old biplanes'.

25 June 1941 saw Gunner Geoffrey Fairs posted to Ayrshire in Scotland where volunteers for the Parachute Regiment and the RAF were being recruited. Geoffrey volunteered for the RAF, was accepted and transferred as an Air Cadet to Scarborough for basic RAF training.

By this time we both knew we were made for each other and in July 1941 we got engaged. In August Geoffrey was posted to Toronto, Canada for three months preliminary training to become a pilot; this

---

[1] Honourable Artillery Company.

preliminary training was done using old biplanes.

Having satisfactorily finished this training he was sent to Pensacola Florida, USA, for practical flying. He wrote to Doris stating that 'The aircraft here are monoplanes, much better than the cumbersome old biplanes'.

Geoffrey's first entry in his Royal Canadian Air Force Pilots Flying Log Book was made on 29 December 1941; he was flying in a dual operating N3N-1 single-engine aircraft and by the end of the month he had logged in 3.5 hours as a pupil. By 13 January 1942 he had flown solo. He progressed steadily doing several solo flights and by the end of January his log book records him as having flown 21.5 hours dual and 22.5 hours solo. There followed night flying, formation flying, instrument instruction and flying, familiarisation of other aircraft, navigation, and bombing. His last entry whilst at Pensacola was dated 8 June 1942, recording that he had been credited with 60.7 hours dual flying, 104.3 hours flying solo and 75.4 hours as a passenger.

Wedding picture taken on the steps of St Margaret's Church, Leiston, (Photo from Doris Smith)

He then returned to England and was posted to No 2 Training Squadron, C Training Flight, at Little Rissington, Gloucestershire. Geoffrey was somewhat amused when he and all the trainee pilots had to stick in their Pilot's Flying Log Book, as a salutary reminder to them all, the following:

IMPORTANT NOTICE

AN AIRCRAFT CRASHED THROUGH YOUR CARELESSNESS OR DISOBEDIENCE WILL DIVERT WORKERS FROM BUILDING FIGHTERS AND BOMBERS TO REPAIRING TRAINING AIRCRAFT.

(Shades of Douglas Bader perhaps?)

THE ROYAL AIR FORCE

Doris writes:

> We were so much in love that when Geoffrey got back to England we decided we would marry. Arrangements were made and on 31 October 1942 the marriage ceremony took place at St Margaret's Church Leiston. We then stayed with my parents in Leiston. On the rare occasions when I was able to travel to Geoffrey's station we would stay at a local hotel or boarding house.

Training in the Oxford and the Link trainer including going on a course to Docking and cross-country night flying continued until 10 December 1942 when his log book records that he had achieved the necessary standard to be posted to an active service squadron.

On 10 January 1943 his logbook records his being with 224 Squadron in Coastal Command, which was at Beaulieu doing 'take offs and landings' in a Liberator. This familiarisation training continued for some time and it was on 30 March 1943 that he went on his first A/S (anti-submarine) patrol. From 1 April until 24 April 1943 Geoffrey, as 2nd Pilot, was on convoy escort and anti-submarine patrols. The following day the Squadron moved to St Eval in Cornwall and on 30 April, whilst on convoy escort, they were for some reason diverted to Gibraltar and returned the following day carrying out an anti-submarine patrol en route.

The next few months was very much a mixed bag: performing compass swings, radio calibration, air test of aircraft, bombing practice (one time experimental), and other training. All this was interspersed with the occasional anti-submarine patrol. This was not always done from St Eval; there were times when he would be sent to Beaulieu, to do compass swings and air testing of the aircraft.

In January 1944 whilst on a night-time anti-submarine patrol a U-boat was sighted and attacked, using the Leigh Light,[2] but there is, however, no record of the result of

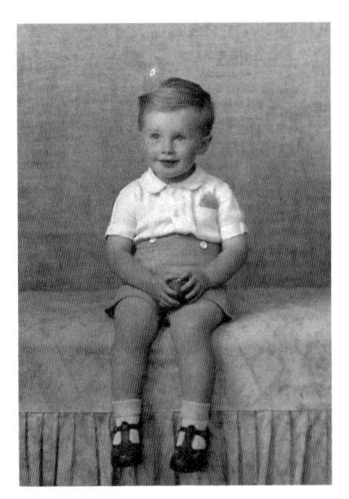

Terry Fairs at age two.
(Photo from Terry Fairs)

---

[2] The Leigh Light was a powerful searchlight used by aircraft, on a final attacking run, to light up a U-boat that had been detected by radar.

96

this attack. The month of May records patrols over the Bay of Biscay but no indication of any actions.

On 24 May 1944 he received the happy news that Doris had given birth to a son whom they named Terence. Geoffrey was overjoyed and was given two days Compassionate Leave to see his newborn son and of course the new mother. The picture opposite shows Terry, as he was soon called, when he was two years old.

Geoffrey's last entry before he was reported missing was of 'Air to air firing' on 30 May 1944. His Pilot's Flying Log Book then shows the bare statement, in red ink: 'Certified missing from operations 6/7th June.'[1944] Signed by the Wing Commander 224 Squadron. Finally, a statement stamped in red: 'DEATH PRESUMED' with another stamp, also in red: 'CENTRAL DEPOSITORY ROYAL AIR FORCE JUL 1946'.

This is a good point at which to explain the lead-up to the loss of Liberator B/224 Squadron and all ten of its crew: Norman Franks, author and air historian has, with Eric Zimmerman, assessed the likelihood of what happened in *U-Boat Versus Aircraft*, using British and German sources. The

Geoffrey (left) with the crew of one of the many Liberators in which he flew. (Photo from Doris Smith)

following account is based on information from their book.

The battle that Geoffrey Fairs's aircraft was involved with on the night of 6/7 June 1944 was the largest single battle between U-boats and aircraft of the entire war. There were inevitably conflicting and confusing reports and it is impossible to give an accurate account of the shooting down of his Liberator. In the darkness, aircraft could not tell which U-boats they were attacking and U-boats found it difficult to identify the aircraft types attacking them.

The task of 224 Squadron, along with other squadrons operating from St Eval, immediately before and during the D-Day landings, was to prevent the massive Allied invasion armada from being infiltrated by German U-boats. To this end Coastal Command filled the sky with aircraft on patrol searching for the enemy.

Fifteen U-boats departed from the French port of Brest on D-Day. Coastal Command lost four aircraft to flak from these U-boats: a Wellington from 407 Squadron, two Liberators from 224 Squadron, and a third from 53 Squadron. The air attacks started at approximately 0130 hours on the morning of 7 June.

In the area where Geoffrey's Liberator was patrolling there were several other aircraft. Geoffrey's Liberator B/224 and a Wellington G/179 were close to one another and encountered three U-boats, U-989, U-415, and U-963. The Wellington saw a U-boat on the surface in one position and at about the same time the Liberator saw another relatively close by.

The last message received from Liberator B/224 was at 0207 stating that it was over a U-boat. At 0212 Wellington G/179 spotted the surfaced U-989. The Wellington found it was too close to attack and swung round to re-position itself. The Liberator B/224 than made a front-gun attack on the U-boat and broke away to starboard. As the Wellington passed overhead and flew away it received flak from the U-boat whilst the aircraft fired both its front and rear guns on the submarine.

As the Wellington flew away it carried out an attack on another U-boat, U-415, dropping a stick of depth charges straddling the submarine amidships. The boat was completely obscured by the explosion and the Wellington encountered no flak as the Liberator B/224 drew the flak fire. The Wellington then heavily strafed the U-boat and as it did came under heavy fire from the third U-boat, U-963. The pilot took evasive action and left the scene. This was at 0225 hours.

By this time Geoffrey's Liberator had positioned itself for yet another

Final notation on Geoffrey's Flying Log Book.
(Photo from Doris Smith)

attack on U-415. The Commander of U-415 reported that at 0228 a Liberator attacked at low altitude from port ahead, dropping four charges. The U-boat's gunners fired back and hit the aircraft, which crashed in the sea. This aircraft was almost certainly Geoffrey Fairs's Liberator B/224. U-415 was severely damaged in the attack and there were many injuries to the crew.

THE ROYAL AIR FORCE

It was only able to operate on a single electric or diesel motor and began the return to Brest submerged to try to avoid further attack.

The names of the aircrew who were in the B/224 Liberator were: Flying Officer R. H. Buchan-Hepburn RAAF, Pilot; Flight Sergeant G. J. H. Fairs, 2nd Pilot; Flight Sergeant B. Hands RAAF; Flight Sergeant A. Kennedy RAAF; Flight Sergeant P. Hogan RAAF; Flight Sergeant H. Earl RAAF; Flight Sergeant J. D. Whitby RAAF; Flight Sergeant L. Barnes; Flight Sergeant M. D. Dickensen RAAF; Sergeant A. Collins.

Most of the events related above are confirmed by a letter that Doris received from the father of Flight Sergeant Whitby. He had received a letter from Mrs Hands, the mother of Flight Sergeant B. Hands. She was told by a Miss Gellaty of St Eval about the last message received from the Liberator. This read, 'We are in grave danger but we are going in to attack.' The letter from Mr Whitby also stated that 'they [the Liberator] put down two U-boats before they crashed and were seen no more' and also '...that the plane went down only 3 miles from St. Nazaire.'

To return to Doris's story:

> I had made my home with my parents at 7 Kitchener Road, Leiston, and I received a priority telegram, written in pencil, on the 7th June from Geoffrey's Wing Commander. It read as follows: 'Regret to inform you that your husband 657007 Flt/ Sgt G. J. H. Fairs is missing as the result of air operations on 7th June 1944, letter follows. [Stop] Any further information will be communicated to you.
> Wing Commander T. W. T. McComb'.
>
> I was distraught, everything was in a whirl – I only knew that I had to get out of the house and look for what I knew not. I just had to get away and think. After some time I returned to the house and my parents tried to comfort me but I was still in deep shock at the news. Our new baby was only two weeks old. I also knew that somebody must tell Geoffrey's parents, but how could I break the news to them? The Fairses were not on the telephone (very few people had private telephones in those days) so my mother and I went to the public call box and we telephoned the vicar of Walberswick, the Rev. A. D. Thompson, AKC, and he passed on the grave news to Mr and Mrs Fairs.

(Tragically another of the Fairses' sons would be lost before the war was over: Sidney John (Jack) Fairs was killed in Italy on 22 April 1945.)

Doris kept hoping and praying that Geoffrey would return or be found but as the time passed hope faded and she braced herself to accept that she would never see Geoffrey again and that he had been killed.

It was inevitable that Doris, a pretty young widow, would eventually attract the young men in Leiston and three years later in 1947 she was married to Leonard Smith. Their marriage was blessed with two daughters and so Terence had not only a new father but also two sisters.

Terry, as he is known, writes of his thoughts:

> I was, of course, at the time too young to realise I had lost my father but was very fortunate my mother remarried someone who brought me up as his own. My mother did, however, keep my Fairs surname which I believe made it easier for me to maintain contact with my natural father's family. I especially remember 'Nana' Fairs making what must have been very tortuous journeys by 'bus from Walberswick to Ipswich and back, where I had my first job, to treat me to lunch and the mannequin parade at Footman's Department Store.
>
> I count myself lucky to have had three sets of grandparents and, as my stepfather also came from a large family, a lot of aunts and uncles not to mention cousins.
>
> Despite our different surnames, I really can't imagine that my relationship with my two sisters and life generally would have been different had we shared both the same parents.

Battle of Britain and onward
John William Bird

John Bird was born in Blythburgh on 13 November 1919. He attended the Blythburgh Primary School until he was 11 and then went on to the Area Council School at Reydon. He had to cycle the eight or so miles on a bicycle provided by the East Suffolk Education Authority. He left school when he was 14, taking a job as a farm labourer for Ernie Heath, a local shopkeeper, who also had a smallholding. Mr Heath was a hard taskmaster. John had to work long hours including Sundays. He was very unhappy, didn't know what to do, and finally decided to run away, which he did, spending a most uncomfortable night at Blythburgh railway station. This ended his employment with Ernie Heath and he was not sorry. He then took a job as a shepherd boy at Henham where he had his own dog called Smokie, and was put in charge of 300 sheep. The pay was ten shillings (50p) a week and this, in 1935, was a good wage for a young lad. A married farm labourer's basic wage was only thirty shillings (£1.50) a week in those days.

In 1936 he changed jobs and worked as a barman at the King's Head, Beccles, until just after war was declared. On 18 September 1939 John enlisted in the RAF at Norwich, aged 19. After being sworn in he was sent to Uxbridge where he received his uniform and was fully equipped. As a raw recruit his first experience of Royal Air Force discipline was not a very happy one for him. The tale he tells, though, is amusing:

> When I first joined up at Uxbridge I felt myself very smart in my uniform and, as I had always been thought rather handsome, I was looking forward to a night out on the town with the ladies. Well, I got to the guardroom all ready to go out when the corporal yelled at me and said, 'Stand to attention. You're not going out like this – your tie isn't straight. Now, go back to your billet and stay there.' I just felt awful. My aspirations to a night out shattered, I returned to my room. This experience really scared me but I suppose they thought I wouldn't be a credit to the RAF.
>
> I was very green in those days – after all I had only been a shepherd boy. So when I was told that we were to salute anyone wearing a peaked hat, well I even saluted the postman who was delivering mail to the barracks.
>
> From Uxbridge I was posted to Cardington, Bedfordshire, to do basic training and when this was over I was sent to a Blenheim squadron at Digby where I worked on the petrol bowsers refuelling the planes with aviation fuel.
>
> I vividly recall one incident when we had just refuelled a Blenheim. It was loaded with bombs and ammunition and waiting for take-off. My mate, who smoked a pipe, had a petrol lighter which had run dry so he refilled it with the aviation fuel that was dripping from the hose. He then, automatically, tried to light it. Luckily the flint must have got wet so it didn't spark. My reactions though were swift and I knocked the lighter from his hands before he tried again and succeeded in blowing up the Blenheim and us.
>
> Shortly after this, in May 1940, our Squadron, the 229th (11 Group), converted to Hurricanes and we were sent to Wittering for

familiarisation and training and getting ready for the Battle of Britain – though of course at the time we didn't know it would be called that. We stayed there until late August or early September 1940. Then the Squadron was posted to Northolt, London.

At Northolt I worked at the end of the runway in a big wooden hut where the pilots were all ready for takeoff. There was a table there with a direct telephone link to the operations room. It was my job to take messages, pass them on to the pilots, and enter them in the logbook. At the word 'Scramble – Angels 15, patrol base' the pilots would dash to their aircraft take off and patrol the base at 15,000 feet. Once they were in the air they would get a radio message from Operations telling them where the German planes were and how many. Our planes would then return and upon landing would refuel and re-arm and up and away they would go again. They were continuously going up and down, and away. We had two Flights, 'A' Flight and 'B' Flight, and they would interchange. When one Flight had done its stint or was exhausted and had had enough, the other would take over. A lot of the pilots were young University people wearing their scarves and they seemed as if they didn't give a damn and we were always losing planes. The losses were such that we constantly had not only to replace planes but pilots as well.

John, with pal, inspecting a crashed German plane found in the desert. (Photo from John Bird)

THE ROYAL AIR FORCE

According to *Battle of Britain* by Richard Townshend Bickers, during the officially recognised period of the Battle of Britain, 10 July to 31 October 1940, of the 41 aircrew assigned to 229 Squadron, 14 aircrew were killed and one died – a loss rate of 34%.

During that period I also remember, because I was tall, being called upon to act as pallbearer at the funeral of an airman. This was for something special and I am glad to say that was the only time I was asked to perform this duty.

In the middle of 1941 we were told the Squadron would be going to the desert and we were given four days leave. They kitted us out with khaki drill (KD) uniform and the medics gave us all those jabs. Upon our return from leave we were sent to Greenock and embarked on a Dutch ship called the *Christiana Hoagan,* a liner. By the time they got us all on the ship was chock-a-block and we left Greenock at night in convoy bound for Freetown. Well I was okay, I am a good sailor but some of the others had never seen a ship before and many of them were

Standing by a tank knocked out in one of the many battles in the Western Desert. (Photo from John Bird)

violently seasick. We slept in hammocks on a deck below the water line. When you went to the toilet it was a great effort to get back into the hammock. The toilets were extremely unpleasant. With so many being seasick the smell was awful and the deck slippery with vomit.

Although we were in a convoy, we were bombed just before we got to Freetown and the ship was hit. The bomb made a fair sized hole and we had to stay in Freetown for eighteen days while they put concrete in the hole as an emergency repair. All the time we were waiting for the repair to be completed we lived on the ship. It was so hot and we spent a most unpleasant eighteen days there, not helped by the knowledge of the conditions in which the officers were living. They were on the top deck with its fans going and they were swigging their gin and tonics. However I do remember at night the wonderful sight of flying fish being surrounded by phosphorescence.

When we got to Durban we were billeted in Clarewood Camp while the ship was being properly repaired. Durban was an astonishing place after wartime Britain. There was no blackout and no rationing. One of our lads went to a shop where they sold sweets and asked the lady how many bars of chocolate he could buy and she said, 'As much as you want'. Nothing was rationed – it was wonderful and the local people were so kind and hospitable.

After the *Christiana Hoagan* had been repaired we re-embarked and set sail up the East Coast of Africa to Alexandria, Egypt. I well remember the awful heat at Aden and the Suez Canal. We were wearing our KD by then and were allowed, in the daytime, to go on the top deck where it was much cooler. Even so when we lay down on the deck the heat and humidity was such that when you got up you left behind a pool of water where you had been lying.

One can imagine what it must have been like having to sleep in the cramped conditions on the lower deck below the water line in all that heat and with inadequate ventilation. It is no wonder that John and his comrades kept comparing their conditions with those of the officers. But considering the circumstances there was little, if anything, that could have been done at that time to improve their situation.

Upon our arrival at Alexandria we disembarked and assembled at Heliopolis where we were issued with our desert equipment. From there we moved to a desert airfield. Our planes were already there having been flown out direct. The Squadron's mission was to give front-line fighter support to our troops and in particular the tanks.

This was at the time when General Wavell was there and the Germans had pushed our troops back. After General Auchinleck took over they advanced and I remember, after one particular battle, having to help bury the dead. There were New Zealand, British, and also German dead. There were so many we could only give them a temporary shallow grave and had to bury them with a part of the leg sticking out so we could easily locate them and bury them properly later on. By the time we had completed this gruesome task we were dog-tired and glad to get some sleep. We awoke the following morning and found the nomad Arabs had gone through the lines during the night, undetected by our sentries, and had taken the boots and socks off every one of the corpses. They were eventually given a proper burial.

This brings to my mind an occasion when a German officer had been killed. His head was hanging out of the turret of a tank and round his neck was a pair of binoculars. A Sergeant-Pilot who was with me said he would like to have the binoculars but couldn't bring himself to take them off so asked me to get them for him. I did so and handed them over to him. The next day the Sergeant-Pilot took off in his Hurricane and was shot down. He bailed out, but his parachute failed to open and he was killed. This incident reminded me sharply of my mother telling me that you should never rob the dead.

John (left) with his friend in Cairo (Photo from John Bird)

In August 1942 General Montgomery arrived and took

Command of the Eighth Army and the battle of El Alamein followed.

Our Squadron was based close by, at a place called Amariha near the coast with a railway running through it. Flies and scorpions there beset us, making living conditions almost intolerable. The water ration was only one gallon per man per day and this was for everything. We got just one pint for drinking. The rest went for cooking and washing. The food was monotonous: we had bully beef and biscuits for breakfast, bully beef and biscuits for dinner, and bully beef and biscuits for tea. The cooks did their best mixing the bully beef with the hard biscuits making it into a sort of stew. Now and then we would get the rare treat of a tin of fruit or something else. On rare occasions we had a chance to get back to Cairo and it was great to be able to have a good wash and some decent food. Yet, in spite of all this we all kept very fit.

John in uniform, showing his Air Gunner Badge and North Africa Star ribbon with rosette. (Photo from John Bird)

I remember going to Cairo after the Battle of El Alamein. This was the first time the British Army had had a major victory and I attended a thanksgiving service in the Cathedral where we sang the hymn, 'The strife is o'er the battle won'. This was a most appropriate hymn and it was wonderful to hear it.

There came a time when more air-crew were needed, so I volunteered. I was sent to Bulawayo, Southern Rhodesia, now Zimbabwe, for air gunnery training where I passed out and got my brevet. When we left to go to our new assignments we were sent by train to Durban. There we were issued with passports and civilian clothes. We were allowed to choose a complete outfit from a store there. This gave us the idea that we were going back to England; instead, we were sent to Egypt. They put us on a Sunderland to fly back to Cairo but because the Sunderland didn't have the range to get there in one hop we had to go back through Mozambique [Portuguese East Africa], a neutral country and land there to be refuelled. The journey took some time and we stopped at several places. When we were in Mozambique I tried crocodile meat. We landed on Lake Victoria in Uganda, and went to a hotel in Kampala where a blind man was playing the *Warsaw Concerto* on the piano; it was a poignant and emotional moment for me.

When we got back to Egypt I remember going into the hangar and crewing up. I was now a Sergeant air gunner. We formed a crew and were given a trial run on a Wellington bomber dropping leaflets over Crete. When on a leaflet raid bomb aiming equipment is not used, the leaflets are just thrown out. We had to fly three times round the target area and by the third circuit the Germans knew where we were heading. After this raid we crashed on landing and the plane was a write off. I was in the rear turret and landed about 300 yards away from the rest of the plane – luckily I was unhurt. The front gunner, however, had been thrown from his seat and was found sitting on the seat of the Elsan toilet. We were checked over by the Medical Officer who said we were only shaken up. We were ordered to get into another plane and take off again immediately, to do 'circuits and bumps' so we wouldn't lose our nerve.

Between Port Said and Alexandria planes could fly at 10,000 feet and the British ack-ack wouldn't touch us but if you happened to go over the Fleet the Navy would fire on you unless you showed the colours of the day. One time, when we came back from a leaflet raid on Crete and because of bad navigation, we came in over the Fleet at Alexandria. The Navy switched on their searchlights and the ack-ack opened up until our navigator fired the current colours of the day – immediately the guns went silent and the searchlight went out. This was a terrifying experience and we told our navigator what we thought of him. We returned to base congratulating ourselves on how fortunate it was that we had returned safely.

During our time in the desert we would go up and down as the battlefront moved to different places and my Squadron, the 229th, eventually split up. Some went to Malta and others to Mersa Matruh. I had a pal, a school friend, Spud Janes from Blythburgh, who was in Malta and I wrote him an uncensored letter and asked one of the pilots who was going to Malta to deliver it. As he came over Malta he was shot down and killed. My letter was found and taken from his body and I got a right good rollicking for that. The pilot was an American and he was one of many taking Hurricanes to reinforce Malta's defences.

I remember being at Mersa Matruh and taking part in a boxing match for the 117th Squadron against the 17th SAAF. My opponent was a big black man from South Africa. I did my best for the Squadron, but I really didn't stand a chance and he knocked me out in the third round.

Signpost in the middle of the Western Desert. (Photo from John Bird)

My next posting was to a Liberator Squadron of the 31st SAAF at Foggia, which was flying missions over Italy and I had quite a time while I was with them.

At one time our engineer had been a bit careless about levelling out the fuel in the tanks and we had an engine cut out because the petrol supply was disrupted. Another time we were flying over hilly terrain when the radio caught fire. It was at night and we were given the order to bail out. Our crew had never been told what to do if we had to bail out so the whole crew refused to do so and told the pilot to try and get us home. Lady Fortune must have been smiling on us because we got home safely.

Cartoon of the 'D-Day Dodgers'. One of the well-known WW II 'Two Types' cartoons by Jon.

It was at this time that a Liberator with all my friends on board exploded and when we returned I was told to report to the office where they asked me to identify the crew. This was a sickening task as the explosion had dismembered all the bodies. The shock of seeing my friends like that upset me so much that I refused to fly again. Our bomb aimer, navigator and front gunner, all friends together, did the same. We were all given a court martial and I was stripped of my sergeant's stripes and reduced to the rank of corporal.

In 1944 those of us who were in Italy at the time of the D-Day landings were known as 'The D-Day Dodgers' and a song was made up about this to the tune of *Lili Marlene*. We always thought this was rather unfair as we were busy fighting in another theatre of war and not everyone could have taken part in the Normandy landings.

The Desert Air Force, of which John was a member, was recognised by

Field-Marshal Montgomery in his farewell speech to the Eighth Army when he was appointed Commander of the 21st Army Group preparing for the D-Day landings in Normandy:

> I am also very sad at parting from the Desert Air Force. This magnificent air striking force has fought with the Eighth Army throughout the whole of its victorious progress; every soldier in this Army is proud to acknowledge that the support of this strong and powerful air force has been a battle-winning factor of the first importance. We owe the Allied Air Forces in general, and the Desert Air Force in particular, a very great debt of gratitude.[3]

When John was at Naples the time came for him to go home, but he injured his knee whilst playing a friendly game of football and spent some time in hospital and had to watch the troopship he should have been on sailing home without him. He finally arrived in Southampton after four and a

Marchpast of the RAF Association at Acton, London.
(Photo from John Bird)

[3] Bernard Law, Viscount Montgomery of Alamein, *The Memoirs of Field-Marshal Montgomery*, Collins, St James Place, London 1958, p. 206.

half years overseas and went to church to give thanks for his safe return. He then collected his kit and got drunk.

John was awarded five medals and two bars. Whilst in the desert he caught malaria spondylitis, caused by a parasite of the same name, and also suffered from a dislocated neck. He applied for a war pension for these complaints but was unsuccessful.

He was married at Southwold on 10 July 1945 to Dorothy Barber, whose father was the Piermaster. Finally, in January 1946 he went to Cardington where he got his de-mob suit. The 'shepherd boy' had done his duty for King and Country.

John's interesting experiences did not end when the fighting was over and he writes as follows:

> After the war we had the Alamein Reunion in the Albert Hall on the anniversary of the Battle of El Alamein, October 23rd.
>
> As we walked into the Albert Hall there was a bar set up for the Air Force then another bar for the 10th Armoured Division and another for the Gurkhas. I went to the RAF bar where I bought a crate of beer, as did all my friends. The reunion itself was for men only though there were serving female soldiers helping to run the event. As I walked in to get a programme and a free packet of Senior Service cigarettes, a girl I went to school with, Jessie Rose, was dishing them out. She recognised me and slipped me an extra packet.
>
> After the speeches and everything, there was a march past and I particularly remember the Gurkhas getting a fantastic cheer from everybody.

This is really the end of John's wartime stories, but the following two tales reflect his character so well that the compilers have included them.

One tells of his involvement with Mobbs Mayhew, a well-known Southwold character, and the rescue of people stranded down Ferry Road, Southwold during the dreadful floods of 1953. The other is closely allied to the war, also with Mobbs Mayhew and his brother Stork, when they caught a live land-mine in their draw net and John informed the police and helped drag it to a safe place until the bomb disposal people dealt with it. He recalls:

> I was in the Sole Bay Inn and met Mobbs Mayhew who had been drinking in The Nelson. He said 'Boy (he always called me that), there are some people that are stranded down Ferry Road, what are we going

to do about it?' I said, 'Well, it's up to you.' So he said, 'Look, I've got my fishing boat down by the pier.' Stanley Townshend, who was with us and worked at Cricks the coal merchant, had a flat lorry so Mobbs said, 'Stanley, get your lorry and we'll see you down the pier. You and me, boy, will go down to the Pier and get the boat.' Having got to the pier Stanley then arrived with the lorry so Mobbs and I got the boat up to it and the three of us managed to heave it on to the back of the lorry with its two sets of oars. 'Don't forget to put the bung in, boy' said Mobbs, 'otherwise we'll bloody sink.' So that was hammered home and we got down to Ferry Road. The weather was terrible. We unloaded the boat and got it into the water, Mobbs got in with one set of oars, and I pushed and then jumped in after him with the other set. We both started to row in very high seas and the wind was blowing hard. I soon found out that I didn't have enough experience to help Mobbs in weather like this so he said, 'I think we'd better go back and get somebody else.' There was another fisherman standing nearby; he got in and between them they rescued one lot of Americans, including a babe in arms, standing on the roof of their house and they got them into the boat. When Mobbs came ashore with them his mouth was all froth with the exertion of fighting the wind and waves. He had the baby in his arms and he said to me, 'Boy, I want a cup of tea', so I went to the cottage where they were making teas and got him a boiling hot cup. He slurped it right down and said, 'Thank God for that.' And with that they pushed off again and rescued some more people on a roof further down the Ferry Road. Those were brought safe to shore and as there were no more people waiting to be rescued Mobbs said, 'Come on boy let's go home – bugger the boat we'll leave that till tomorrow.' So we all went home.

My home was in Reydon and Southwold had been cut off by the floods so as my father-in-law, Mr Barber, lived in a house in Victoria Street the missus and me stayed there. I was soaking wet and couldn't get a change of clothes so continued wearing these until they dried out. We had left the dog at home in Reydon and we just hoped he was all right.

Some time later Mobbs Mayhew was awarded a well-deserved BEM, which was presented to him by the Earl of Stradbroke. I also went and received letters of thanks from the Council.

Mobbs Mayhew was the most wonderful man I ever met in my life.

THE ROYAL AIR FORCE

One evening he, his brother Stork, a retired fisherman, and I were having a drink in The Nelson and after the pub closed Mobbs said, 'Come on boy we'll go down the beach and do a bit of drawing.' With drawing a long net is used and I would stand on the beach holding it secure and the boat with the other end attached would come round and make a sweep. It was a moonlight night and the tide was about to come in. We made the sweep and pulled it all in. Suddenly Mobbs said, 'Boy look out, watch that bloody thing there, if you stand on that you'll get blown to smithereens.' I took one look and said, 'By God, it's a mine, a live mine.' So I got it down and Mobbs and Stork said I had better report it to the police and they decided to go home leaving me to it. This was about one or two o'clock in the morning. So I went to knock on Police Inspector Moore's door. He wasn't very happy being woken up at that hour, but I said, 'There's a mine way back on the beach and the tide's coming in.' So he said, 'Okay', and he got his car out with ropes and everything and said, 'Come on, show me where it is.' We went down to the pier and then up on the way nearly to Covehithe. There was the mine the water just lapping over it. Inspector Moore said, 'Well we've got to do something about it. We can't go away and leave it here, the two of us.' I said, 'Oh dear, I've only just got back from the bloody war.' Inspector Moore said, 'We'll get the rope, Mr Bird, and you can help me drag it up the beach.' On the mine was a kind of trip-trigger thing and of course the waves were lifting this trigger thing up and down and we were trying to get the rope under the damn mine without touching the trigger. I was behind the Inspector and finally we got the rope right and he said, 'You'd better get behind me in case it blows up.' 'Well', I said, "if it blows up I'm a goner anyway.' He got round me so he was in front and said, 'Right. Action.' Well, I was sweating – I was terrified. Anyway we managed to get it above the high-water mark and he rang up the Bomb Disposal people and they came and blew it up. Well you never heard such a noise in all your life. I went home and my missus said, 'Oh there's been an explosion down on the beach.' I said, 'I know. I was there.' Later on I got a letter of thanks from the Chief of Police for the assistance I had given to Inspector Moore that night.

John told many more interesting tales but they are outside the scope of this book. Perhaps someone who is looking for Suffolk tales will include them in such a book. We hope so.

One WAAF's wartime experience
Nancy Ellen Osborne, née Rogers

Nancy, or Nan as she likes to be called, was born and bred in Walberswick and lived in Ferry Knoll, a cottage on Ferry Road. Her father was George Rimmington Rogers, a well-known character in the village. He owned a garage and a lock-up shop on the village green where he sold ironmongery, bicycles, and fishing tackle. This business remained in the family until the spring of 1970. The garage is now a restaurant and the lock-up a wine shop – such is progress. Her mother was Rosamund Rogers, née Youngs, who came from Wangford.

Nan had an older sister Dorothy and a brother, named after his father – George Rimmington – and his story is recorded in Chapter 2.

Nan in her WAAF uniform.
(Photo from Nan Osborne)

Nan writes:

> I left school in 1935 and went to work at Griffins, a shop selling ladies wear and soft furnishings in Southwold. I then went to live with my sister Dorothy at Wallingford in Berkshire and it was from there that I enlisted as an ACW (Aircraft Woman) in the WAAF (Women's Auxiliary Air Force), on 11 December 1941. They sent me to Insworth Lane, Gloucester, to be kitted out and do my basic RAF training. Having completed this I was posted to Morecambe where I was given further training and then sent to Bridlington on a career training course, which lasted from January 1942 until March of that year.
>
> My training completed, I was posted to the 12th Operational Training Unit (OTU) at Chipping Warden, Oxfordshire, as an Equipment Assistant. There we dealt with all sorts of supplies and equipment including aircraft spares, tools, clothing, petrol, and aviation fuel.

Most of the WAAFs worked in the Main Stores stocking and issuing all the equipment and supplies and dealing with all the considerable amount of paper work this entailed. All issues and receipts had to be recorded and the records kept in large loose-leaf ledgers.

In addition to these routine duties, one night a week two of the girls were detailed as storekeepers and had to sleep in the stores so as to be available to issue and receive tankers of aviation fuel. All the tankers had to be dipped on arrival to record the amount of fuel they were carrying and then again after the delivery to confirm they were empty. To do the dipping we had to climb on top of the tanker, which was rather difficult and in frosty weather could be dangerous. Sometimes we would be called upon two or three times during the night to perform this task. We were not given time off the next day after being on call those nights to catch up on our sleep, only one hour off for a late breakfast and then back to work again.

It was from Chipping Warden that a number of 1,000-plane bomber raids operated and many crews from our camp went on them. Not all the crews that took part in these raids were fully trained and it shows how desperate we were in those days.

Nan's memory hasn't let her down, for it was on the night of 30 May 1942 under Operation MILLENNIUM that the first 1,000-bomber raid took place and Cologne was the target. Air Marshal Sir Arthur (Bomber) Harris had scraped together 1,047 aircraft (at that time the greatest fleet of aircraft that had ever been assembled). Incendiary as well as high explosive bombs were used with devastating effect. Some 3,300 buildings were destroyed and about 470 people killed. Forty-one aircraft and their crews never got back to their base in England.

Then in March 1943 a Wellington bomber (Wimpy) crashed on our WAAF site very near to the hut where I lived. We were very fortunate that no WAAFs were injured but sadly all the aircrew except the rear gunner was killed.

In 1943 I was posted to 1657 Conversion Unit at Stradishall (now the home of Highpoint Prison) where Stirling heavy bombers were stationed.

Then in 1944 I was sent to Chedburgh, near Bury St. Edmunds, Suffolk, with the 1653 Conversion Unit, a satellite of Stradishall, where I was made Corporal in charge of a Flight Stores supplying spares for Lancaster bombers. These Flight Stores were situated on the other side of the airfield, some considerable distance from our Nissen hut and usually fairly near to a hangar. To get there we would have to cycle round the perimeter track. I was very fortunate in that I had been issued with a bicycle; my friend also had one but she couldn't ride so I had to teach her. Our job was to keep all spares and tools stocked up from the Main Stores and issue them to the fitters and flight mechanics, as they were required; all the tools had to be signed out on loan. Another job was to issue the fitters and mechanics with clean overalls once a week.

I cannot remember there being any serious air raids on the camp but the area around Chedburgh had its fair share of doodlebugs (V1s, flying bombs); here again we were very lucky and we had no WAAF casualties.

I was at Chedburgh when the build-up to D-Day began and during this time we had to work extremely hard. The hours were long: 8 a.m. to 10 p.m. each day working seven days a week with no time off whatsoever and this continued for many weeks. The conditions under which we lived didn't help either but we stuck at it.

The living conditions in the wartime camps were primitive and made life quite hard. The Nissen huts were heated by Tortoise Stoves, which we found difficult to light and fuel was scarce. It was a very long walk to get to the cookhouse and to the ablutions, and hot water was rarely available. The baths had no plugs and so we provided our own; they were plugs which fitted all sizes of plugholes.

Then in 1945 the complete unit moved to RAF North Luffenham in Rutland and whilst I was there on 8 June 1945 the *London Gazette* announced that I had been awarded a Mention in Dispataches.'

Nan believes this award was in recognition of all the hard work and long hours, under difficult conditions she had to endure during the run-up to D-Day. Nan was finally demobbed in March 1946 at Wythall, Birmingham, and returned to Walberswick.

Nan completes her story:

It was in October 1945 when I was stationed at North Luffenham that I met and fell in love with Flying Officer, Harold William (Red) Osborne who was also stationed there. Some time later he was moved and posted to Mepal in Cambridgeshire where in August 1946 he was demobbed. We then were married and in September 1946 he took a job as a pilot with British European Airways (BEA), which later became British Airways. We were blessed with two sons, Laurence and Timothy.

Red retired 31 years later in September 1977 as a Senior Training Captain of British Airways. After his retirement we lived at Farnham Common, Buckinghamshire, and in 1979 moved to Blythburgh. With Red's health failing we decided to move to Farnham, Surrey, in order to be nearer to our family. Sadly Red died on 24 May 1998.

Chapter 4
THE MERCHANT NAVY

Convoys In home waters
Arthur George Clarke

In Chapter 27 of the book *Dried Egg and Doodlebugs*,[1] Arthur describes the country as:

> bristling with uniformed men and women of different Services and nationalities...and other good organisations. Intermingled with these seething masses were a vast number of men unnoticed and unrecognised by the general public, who were gallantly adding their contribution to the War effort.... These men were not and never have been acclaimed for what they did to serve the country. They were attired in civilian clothes, usually dark in colour with a roll neck jumper rather than a collar and tie. They had not sworn allegiance to the King and Country. Neither had they need to, they were following their normal profession and were fiercely patriotic with deep national pride. Classed as civilians, they were men of the Merchant Navy. Their only means of identification was a small silver badge worn in the lapel, a wreath of leaves surrounding the letters MN. They carried a special identity card, which bore all their personal details and their fingerprints – just enough details to identify a body if found to be floating at sea. Officers did have a uniform similar to that of the Royal Navy, probably because they had to work closely with them. There was a briefing before any convoy left port. The Navy would plan and guide the convoy, placing a senior Officer aboard a designated merchant ship, the 'Commodore Ship'. This ship would lead the other merchant ships in the convoy to their destination. Life aboard was hard with very little comforts and no matter what the weather they had to carry on.

---

[1] *Dried Egg and Doodlebugs*, The Pattemore Pen Pushers, Pendragon, Stradbroke, Eye, Suffolk, 1995.

Normally, seamen had very little choice of which ships they would prefer to join. A 'Stand-by' system existed whereby men would be paid a little extra to be on immediate call – no choice given. Ships sailed to a tight schedule – last minute illness or accident often raised a need for an immediate replacement.

Such a person was Arthur Clarke, born in Blythburgh in 1922. He attended the Elementary Schools at Blythburgh and Wenhaston. Upon leaving school in 1937 he obtained work at the Empire Pool Wembley (part of the Wembley Stadium complex). In 1938 he returned to Blythburgh and in 1939 took a summer job as a Walls ice cream salesman in the area. (The Walls ice cream tricycle painted dark blue with the sign 'Stop me and buy one' was a familiar sight in those days.) After war was declared he signed-on on the steam drifter *Foresight* fishing out of Lowestoft around the coast of Fleetwood and the Irish Sea. This did not last too long; the Royal Navy commandeered the vessel to serve as a Barrage Balloon ship outside various British ports. He writes:

Arthur wearing his silver Merchant Navy badge on his lapel, the only bit of uniform the ordinary Merchant Seaman wore. Officers, however, did have a uniform.
(Photo from Arthur Clarke)

> During the early part of the war I was on colliers – coal ships, trading from London to Blyth, Northumberland, up and down the East Coast carrying coal from the Tyne to the London Gas Works. The shipping lane, known as 'E Boat Alley', was a virtual graveyard for coastal ships of up to 5,000 tons. I saw action at dusk when E Boats attacked the convoys and again at dawn when the dive-bombers attacked. This was practically an everyday occurrence particularly in 1942. At one

time I was in a convoy which left the Thames with twenty-seven ships and arrived in the Tyne with only thirteen.

One wintry Sunday afternoon the convoy was on stand-by alert. Steaming north we had all guns pointing out to sea ready for the expected attack. At dusk it came – but from behind us. The Germans had brazenly crossed the North Sea in daylight and laid in wait for us, inside the Yarmouth Roads. Our losses were heavy as we were caught off guard.

I signed on the *Prestatyn Rose,* a coasting vessel until I was taken ill and had to leave. Once I was well enough I signed on the SS *Mirupanu*, with my brother George, as an Able Seaman.

On one voyage just off the Humber, aircraft attacked the *Mirupanu* and a bomb hit her; luckily none of the crew was hurt and our gunner shot the plane down. This attack put us in Immingham Dock for eleven weeks undergoing repairs. I served on this ship for two years and 1943 saw me on yet another trading vessel the SS *Cherbourg.*

The opportunity arose shortly after to change to a larger and better ship the MV *Empire Ness* but she was still trading in the same waters. I missed joining her and she sailed from Grimsby without me. I arrived at the dock just in time to see her steaming out to sea. It was not my fault for missing my ship; the train I was on from Ipswich to Grimsby was caught in an air raid going across the Fens and had to stop and dampen down its fires. By the time we reached Grimsby it was too late. I, as a civilian, was brought before the local Court, fined £1 and put on the 'Stand-by' list. This meant I had no choice of ship but had to take the first berth I was offered.

Crew members often 'missed their ship'. It was a common occurrence and happened mostly through drunkenness, domestic trouble at home, illness, sheer bravado, et cetera. Although we were civilians there had to be some discipline and 'Missing Ship became a Statutory Offence and a £1 fine was the normal punishment. Persistent offences of this nature would, as a last measure, result in spending a few weeks in prison. Every Seaman had a personal discharge book, which recorded his movements in the Merchant Navy. It was stamped with the ship's stamp when a man signed on and when he was paid off. In order that a Seaman would not attract a criminal tag for such an offence it was strongly rumoured that after a spell in prison a man's Discharge Book would bear the stamp HMS *Durham*.

Arthur eventually served on the *Empire Ness* and explains that merchant seamen remained in the employ of the ship's owner and that was why they were regarded as civilians.

> In 1944 the War Office commandeered the *Empire Ness* to be used as a supply vessel backing up the landings in Normandy. Meanwhile I had volunteered for 'Special Services' and was serving in her when she was at Arromanches on D-Day following up the troops. She was loaded with supplies and armaments for our forces as they went ashore.
>
> The cargo was unloaded by military personnel into landing barges and into the DUKWs (vehicles shaped like a boat with propellers and wheels so they could drive either on land or sea), which plied from ship to shore. I foolishly persuaded one of the DUKW's drivers to get me ashore. This was about 11.30 a.m. and heavy fighting was still going on all around and there were land mines everywhere. I was able to explore the vast concrete gun emplacements and defences the enemy had constructed and I was lucky to come away unscathed.
>
> The *Empire Ness* was later sunk, I think by a mine, in the river Scheldt en route for Ghent, the capital of East Flanders. Happily she settled down on a sandbank allowing all hands, including my brother George, to get away safely. I lost most of my gear, which was still on board.
>
> (When a ship is sunk by enemy action the crews' pay ceased from the time the ship goes down. Any survivors were picked up and brought back to these shores; they would get three weeks survivor's leave with normal pay and put on the Shipping Pool to be given a berth in another ship. A fund existed to give financial help to replace personal belongings consigned to 'Davy Jones' Locker' following the sinking of a ship.)
>
> I was then transferred for a short time to the SS *Greta Force* and then to the MV *Kemball Harlow*, both of them on special operations supplying the troops. After D-Day whenever we were returning to the UK we would sometimes bring back German prisoners of war.
>
> In 1945 I was transferred to the MV *Royal Daffodil*, this time ferrying troops from the Continent to Dover.

After the war Arthur had the honour of being selected one of only four men who represented the Merchant Navy on the parade in the Albert Hall

The MV Royal Daffodil *leaving the Continent loaded with troops bound for Dover.*
(Photo from Arthur Clarke)

where the Empire Festival of Youth was held.

He obtained his discharge from the Merchant Service in 1946 and re-entered the fishing industry doing long-shore fishing from Southwold beach.

Since then he has, through sheer hard work and determination, become a very successful businessman. He commenced farming, purchasing two farms at Hinton, Red House and Red Cap, and founded two companies, Clarke Development Corporation Plc (CDC Demolition Ltd.) and the Land and Leisure Group Ltd. (CDC Landscapes Ltd., Greensports Ltd., and Waldringfield Heath Golf Club Ltd.). He is now retired but still likes to keep involved.

He has also recently made contact with a few of his old Blythburgh school friends and they meet occasionally to have a meal and talk about the old days.

Arthur had three brothers who also served during the war: George, Frank, and Jack. Sadly all three have died but Arthur does have some information as to what they did during the war:

George joined the Royal Navy as a boy of 15 and did his training in HMS *Warspite*, then went into the Merchant Navy. When war broke out he was in the London Fire Brigade until 1940 but the call of the sea was too great for him to resist and he went back to the Merchant Navy.

Frank was called up and served in the Army. Arthur has no idea what regiment he was in or where he served but some time in 1943 Frank was discharged as being unfit for further service.

Jack was also called up in the Army but again there are no details of the Regiment in which he served. He was in the retreat to Dunkirk, was evacuated safely back to England and remained in the Army until the end of the War.

Chapter 5

FLIGHT FROM MALTA

A family escapes
From an original story by Lady Mallaby

Elizabeth Brooke was born in Mexico in 1911. When the First World War broke out it was thought it would be over very shortly. However, when her father realised that his bachelor friends who had joined up were being killed, he decided he must join up himself. The only Regiment which would accept a man at the age of 46 was the Artists' Rifles. His wife insisted that if he went she and the family should go with him. They sailed on a French ship, the SS *Navarre*, bound for France. Off the coast of Spain the ship was torpedoed, but they eventually made their way to Biarritz, France, from where he intended to make his way to England to join his Regiment. However this was not to be, for on 16 December 1916 he died very suddenly of angina. Elizabeth's mother and the four children had to stay until the end of the war and then made their way to England, where they lived throughout her schooldays. In 1932 she sailed to Tanganyika to help her sister who was expecting her second child. Elizabeth had met James (Jim) Locker, a young colonial officer, on board the ship, and they eventually married in Dar

Elizabeth Locker in her later days as Lady Mallaby.
(Photo by Miriam Dillon)

125

es Salaam in 1934. They had three children, Anne, Judy, and Timothy. The story commences:

> My husband, Jim Locker, who had been appointed Assistant to the Lieutenant Governor (later Government Chief Secretary), myself and three children, aged 4, 2 and 1, arrived in Malta in April 1939. We took up residence in an old Maltese house, No. 101 Strada Reale, above a large sunken garden on the edge of the sea at Balluta Bay, St Julians. An enchanting house but very inconvenient, with huge windows (difficult to black out), tile floors, and a stone staircase.
>
> Hall, dining room, and kitchen were downstairs, and upstairs four bedrooms, nursery, and bathroom, all leading off the drawing room, and two flat roofs.
>
> Mussolini declared war on 10 June 1940 and the next day we had the first air raid, which the children, nanny, and I saw from the flat roof of our house. We watched the dog fight between the Italian *Regia Aeronautica* fighter planes and three old Gloster Sea Gladiators, hastily unpacked from their crates as no fighter planes had reached Malta. It was an extraordinary sight – puffs of white cotton-wool-like smoke from the anti-aircraft guns and the three lumbering old Gladiators, bumbling about like huge moths with the Italian planes circling around and a distant sound of gunfire. There was no feeling of fear, I remember; it all seemed so unreal. It was a very different story later in

Anne sitting with the nanny, Mrs Hunter. (Photo from Lady Mallaby)

the day when we had our first proper air raid with some ten *Savoia Marchetti*, SM79 three-engine Italian planes bombing Valletta and the coast, inflicting the first casualties (some 100 people were killed). After this, air raids became more frequent, but it was not until the Luftwaffe took over in December that the raids became heavier and more damaging. It was too dangerous to stay in our old house right on the edge of Balluta Bay so, having discovered an old wine cellar under the house, we went to stay with friends until the Public Works Department could reinforce the roof, make an escape tunnel into the garden and build a steep wooden stair down from the dining room. The cellar was dark and damp, but reasonably safe apart from a direct hit. We had acquired a Maltese Terrier called Rex who was later to prove a great asset. He not only heard the approach of enemy planes before the air raid warning sounded but he also seemed to be able to tell the difference between the Allied and enemy bombers and ran straight to the shelter. This gave us an extra few seconds to dash to the shelter ourselves. He never made a mistake.

Rex, the Maltese terrier. (Photo from Lady Mallaby)

The only air defence Malta had when the Italians declared war was 42 anti-aircraft guns and the Gloster Gladiators biplanes referred to above. There were actually four of these planes but one of them was soon damaged in action and written off. The remaining three were nicknamed 'Faith, Hope, and Charity'. Eight separate air raids took place that first day, the 11th of June, with 40 bombers and their fighter escorts taking part. Early evening saw the last of the raids on Valletta's naval installation and dockyard. For three weeks Faith, Hope, and Charity faced the enemy alone. There were seven Gladiator pilots who flew in relays and they performed extremely well

FLIGHT FROM MALTA

Above: Port Valletta harbour.
Below: The barbed wire fence over which the children would be handed for a dip in the sea.
(Photos from Lady Mallaby)

against the bombers. These pilots were looked upon as local heroes and their pictures were displayed in shop windows. Four Mk 1 Hurricanes were then flown in to help in the air defence of the island. Then on 31 July 1940 under Operation HURRY the aircraft carrier *Argus* sailed from Gibraltar with 12 fighter planes for Malta. They were released some 200 miles from the island at a point off the coast of Sardinia and became involved in a dogfight as they arrived over Malta Grand Harbour. One plane was shot down and the pilot killed. One Italian pilot was also killed. The story continues:

A FAMILY ESCAPES

*The children waiting to be lifted over the fence after having a dip.
(Photo from Lady Mallaby)*

Below the house and across the road was an Army post behind a barbed-wire entanglement, guarded by the Irish Fusiliers, to whom we used to hand over the three children for a dip in the sea in the heat of the summer. The children would be rushed back to the shelter when the air raid warning sounded *'Aeroplane Talade Adeo'*, 'Air Raid Warning, Take Cover'.

Life went on comparatively normally until in December German Stukas began their first dive-bombing raids; but there was, of course, no social life as such. My husband's office was in the Castille so, if and when he could get away, we used to meet in the Club known as the Snake Pit in Valletta. Getting there from St Julians meant either a lift in an ox wagon or walking and then getting someone to row one across the Marsamuschetto creek. Very tricky if one was caught in an air raid, as I was on one occasion, but worth the effort to meet one's friends and try and keep up some sort of social life. We would pick our way over the ruins watching the incredibly brave people of Malta, living in the Granaries built by the Knights of Malta, carrying on their daily lives.

Enemy attacks continued, and by December 1940 raids of about 70 Italian bombers were commonplace, opposed by only eight or nine British fighters. The Italian bombers were not successful in subjugating Malta or in sinking the ships bringing essential supplies to the besieged island. Indeed British warships and warplanes were harrying German ships supporting troops in North Africa. On 10 December Hitler ordered the intensification of the air offensive by sending the crack *Luftwaffe Fliegerkorps X* (Flying Corps) to Sicily. Their aim was to gain control of the air in the Central Mediterranean, including Malta. This tiny island of only 122 square miles was a thorn in the side of the Axis powers and of great importance to the Allies. Air superiority would have allowed the enemy safe transport of Rommel's newly formed Afrika Korps to Libya and kept them supplied without harassment. The *Fliegerkorps* consisted of high-level bombers, Stuka dive-bombers and, later, Me109 fighters. The Stuka pilots had been trained in anti-shipping strikes and on 10 January 1941 the aircraft carrier HMS *Illustrious* was severely damaged as she carried out escort duties. (See Lady Mallaby's graphic description and further details on page 133.) Two of the merchant ships were sunk and the cruiser HMS *Southampton* badly damaged with eighty of its crew killed. Subsequently HMS *Southampton* had to be sunk by the Royal Navy. On 14 January seventy German bombers from Sicily attacked the Valletta Grand Harbour with the aim of sinking HMS *Illustrious*. Amazingly they only inflicted minor damage. However the port was badly damaged, about 200 other buildings in Valletta were destroyed and over 50 civilians killed. This was the start of a number of attacks, which the Maltese nicknamed the 'Illustrious Blitz'. With the arrival in the theatre of the Me109s the Mark I Hurricanes were completely outclassed and outnumbered and from then on Malta was bombed remorselessly day and night. The courage of all those on the island never faltered and they tried to live as normal a social life as possible.

> Occasionally the Governor and Lady Dobbie would give an official luncheon in one of the magnificent rooms in the Castille, to boost morale and allow key figures, both Maltese and British, to meet. Wonderful occasions but, being on the edge of the Grand Harbour, we were target number one, and should there be an air raid the chandeliers would sway ominously and had we been hit the whole ceiling would have collapsed on us.
>
> The time came when morale at Ta Qali Fighter Base was low, as their hoped-for reinforcements had failed to arrive. Some of us, and others who were left (HMS *Glorious* had left with all the Naval wives), were

asked to make their way to Ta Qali to cheer up the young pilots standing ready in full fighting kit by their fighter planes. When an air raid sounded we women would leap into the slit trenches alongside as they took off, counting them as they flew overhead. It was nerve-wracking and sometimes distressing when some of the chaps you had just been drinking with did not return, and you could see plumes of smoke and hear the noise of exploding bombs in the direction of your home and children, or Valletta where your husband worked.

Sometimes we would be summoned on the 'Grape Vine' to the Submarine Base, HMS *Talbot* in the Lazaretto Creek, by the Commander, Captain G. W. G. Simpson (known as 'Shrimp'), to come and have a drink to welcome home the crew of a submarine expected back from patrol. We stood on the veranda of this old wooden building looking out anxiously to sea along the channel below Fort St Elmo. It was a stirring sight to see a submarine come in and sail up the creek to where we were waiting, with the crew in white jerseys lining the hull on which were painted skulls and crossbones indicating the number of enemy vessels sunk. Alas, some days we waited in vain. Hours passed and 'Shrimp' would be forced to admit that the submarine was lost. The occasion on which the famous submariner David Wanklyn, VC DSO and 2 Bars, in command of HMS *Upholder*, failed to return from patrol was a devastating blow, particularly as it was his last patrol and he had sunk 21 enemy vessels. He was regarded as a hero throughout Malta.

As I have said, there was little social life but we all tried to keep up morale in any way we could. We kept open house for any odd Army, Navy, and Air Force personnel and others, drinking any odd drink that could be found (on rare occasions, whisky brought in from Alexandria by the submarines). It was mostly local wine, Melita at 6d a bottle and the baby's gripe water as a liqueur should a few have stayed on to eat a meagre goat stew. After one such occasion we took some high-ranking officers, all burping happily, up to watch an air raid from the roof as after dinner entertainment, and a damaged German plane flying low, seeing the red tabs, machine-gunned us; a strong reprimand followed from HQ.

We had some of the most hilarious and splendid parties in spite of all the horror, playing 'The Game' a form of charade, acting out a well-known saying. I'll never forget the AOC (Air Vice-Marshal Sammy Maynard), acting out 'The Marshalling Yards of Ham', hitting his hamstrings ferociously and striding up and down. On one occasion he seemed very distracted, pacing up and down the hall and then leaving in a hurry. We learnt later that only four of the expected 12 much-needed Hurricanes being ferried to Malta on the aircraft carrier HMS *Argus,* had arrived. The others, having apparently taken off too early, lost their way and, running out of petrol, failed to arrive. However, in spite of the complete blackout and little food or drink, and immediate danger from raids, I can honestly say those were the best parties I've ever known. I think we all gave of our best, all little jealousies and personal problems forgotten, knowing the peril we were all in.

There were odd gatherings in people's homes, hurried visits to go swimming at Dragonara Palace by kind permission of the Marchese Scicluna, just up the coast from St Julians; a visit to see the famous Baroness Inguanez in her lovely house at Mdina, and visits to the Stricklands – Mabel heroically carrying on publishing *The Times of Malta* throughout the blitz. These were of course in the early days of the war before the German bombers began their deadly raids in December 1940. In that month alone there were 263 air raids over Malta, which gives some idea of the pressure we were under.

During one of these heavy raids when we were carrying the children down to the shelter at night Jessie, our Maltese maid, tripped and dropped Judy, whose head was cut and bleeding badly. I had to carry her up to the bathroom on the first floor by the light of a torch and try to staunch the bleeding with towels or anything I could find. Life in the shelter was very difficult with some twenty of us, including our Maltese neighbours, crowded together in the damp cellar listening to the explosion of the bombs and the big HAA gun of the 10/7th Regiment at Spinola. We could also hear those at St George's and St Andrew's Batteries up the coast trying to protect the two Army Hospitals (clearly marked with red crosses) from deliberate attack by the German Junker 88s.

A particular party I remember was one we gave to celebrate the engagement of Brigadier 'Bouncer' Cox and the local English schoolmistress Sheila (whose surname escapes me). We had hoped to hold the party in the garden, but heavy rain prevented this. The heavy curtains in the drawing room had to be re-hung after cleaning, so I climbed a high wooden ladder (with the maid holding the bottom on the slippery marble floor). Suddenly there was a heavy air raid and she let go in panic and I crashed down, smashing my left kneecap – just half an hour before the party was due to start. Amazingly and unbelievably I was able to carry on with the party and not until the last guest had left at 2 p.m. did the appalling pain hit me and I passed out. No doctor has ever been able to explain this – I can only assume it was the terrific shock. Doctor Bonaro, our local doctor, was called and he whisked me off in his car to the King George V Hospital on the edge of the Grand Harbour (where I had a 2½ hour operation on my kneecap, which was broken in half). It was due to the huge skill of the Maltese surgeon, Peter Paul Debono, that I was saved from being crippled for life. He drilled four holes in my kneecap and wired it together; my friends had found a tough able-bodied [sick-berth attendant] seaman who, after my knee came out of plaster, massaged and pummelled it fiercely preventing any disabling adhesions forming.

In January 1941 the aircraft carrier HMS *Illustrious* escorting a large convoy of desperately needed supplies was subjected to intense attack by German Stuka dive bombers and was severely crippled and set on fire; 126 crew members were killed during the attack. She limped into the Grand Harbour and was thereafter subjected to a further severe attack by the Stukas. I watched one such dive-bombing attack with my husband from the Castille on the edge of the Grand Harbour when, in spite of an intense barrier of anti-aircraft fire having been put up over the Harbour to protect *Illustrious*, the German Stukas dived, sirens shrieking, one after another like a great Catherine wheel, releasing their bombs. The noise was terrific with exploding bombs and heavy anti-aircraft fire. On 23 January, in spite of this, the *Illustrious* managed to slip out of harbour at night, thanks to the magnificent efforts of those who patched her up and made this possible. The three cities around the harbour, Vittoriosa, Senglea, and Cospicua were very severely damaged. Days later I took our Maltese cook Theresa to search the ruins of Vittoriosa for news of her family, but she could find no trace amidst the ruins. When news of an expected convoy got around, family and friends would line the walls of the Grand Harbour

General Scobell (left) with James Locker (centre) and the Vice Governor HE Sir Edward Jackson waiting to receive Lord Gort, the new Governor, in May 1942.

(Photo from Lady Mallaby)

in Valletta, in spite of the peril, to welcome the arrival of relations. Alas, so often they had not survived; even so, a huge cheer would go up as the crippled ships limped into Harbour. It was a deeply moving experience.

At the time of my accident, Anne had seen me fall and started running a high temperature while Judy and Tim were severely shocked when the nursery windows were shattered in the same raid that had scored a direct hit on Balluta Mansions a short way up the road. As the air raids intensified and we were bombed continuously day and night, our family's health and well being were severely tried. Jimmy, my husband, had asthma and was suffering from enormous stress. My knee was still pretty dicey. Anne had not recovered from her illness and had a lump on her neck after falling into the swimming bath at St Anton Palace. Judy had a tender scar on her head from her fall down the air-raid shelter, and had broken her arm badly falling off her tricycle, and Tim had double pneumonia caused by nights in the very damp shelter. Food on the island was now desperately short and we were five useless mouths to feed, so a plan was made that we should be put aboard the first ship available. Meantime we were told to pack up and be ready to leave. One of the Governor's ADCs would ring us up and ask us to dine at St Anton Palace, the Dobbies' official residence. This was the signal that we were about to leave and we would stay with them until the ship was ready to sail. We were there for some 10 days during which time we lived *'en famille'* with the Dobbies; when they entertained food was very sparse and the Dobbies lived a very frugal life. Whilst strolling in the gardens with the children I once picked up a lemon off the ground with which I hoped to wash the children's hair, and I was severely reprimanded by Lady Dobbie for waste of food.

After dinner it was their custom that all guests assembled for prayers, at which General Dobbie would recount the events of the day in a very matter-of-fact way, telling us which places had suffered during the raids, and praying that God would help and protect us: it sounds

The oil tanker Ohio *being supported by two destroyers* Penn *and* Ledbury *heading for harbour August 1942.*

'corny' but was actually deeply impressive. He was a member of the Plymouth Brethren and deeply religious; a great man loved and respected by everyone. When at last the signal came for our departure, we were driven down to the Harbour late at night and boarded the SS *Settler,* a very small merchant ship of the Harrison Line with a Lascar crew. There were no proper quarters, so the Purser turned out of his cabin for me and Anne and Judy, and the 1st Officer did likewise for my husband and Tim. The ship was shabby and dirty with no proper rails, only low ones, so the children could never be out of our sight. The Governor and Lady Dobbie and their daughter Sybil came to see us off at The Grand Harbour during an air raid. Lady Dobbie gave the children a book of *Grimm's Fairy Tales,* which was to be a valuable distraction on such a perilous journey. When we woke in the morning and went on deck, to our great surprise we were flying the Italian Flag and heading west, apparently following the route cleared of mines for incoming convoys. This was a shock as we presumed we would sail east to Alexandria and from there make our way to my sister and her family in Tanganyika. By dawn we were off Point Caglieri, at the southern end of Sardinia, sailing very close to shore when Italian planes swooped down to have a look at us and the two other ships sailing with us in convoy, but unescorted – suspicions were aroused and more enemy planes circled us.

It was then that the Skipper (very keen on his booze) asked me to go up on deck with Judy – dark and curly haired (I was a brunette in those days), and try and look Italian and wave at the enemy planes; Anne and Tim, being fair headed, were to be kept out of sight. My husband took his rifle up on deck (he was a very good shot and used to provide game for the larder when we were in Nyasaland, now Malawi). The skipper then asked me if I spoke Italian; I said, 'no, but French and some Spanish, why?' 'Could I go down to the wireless operation room and listen to intercepted messages between enemy pilots and mainland Sicily?' A very young 'sparks' officer clapped headphones on me, and I made out that the Italian reconnaissance planes were reporting three suspicious ships east of Point Cagliari and would reconnoitre further. Shortly after, two enemy planes swooped low over us, and I heard them report back that there were no known Italian ships in that area – so they would proceed to harass the enemy. I warned the skipper of impending attack; the crew mustered and got two old Bofors guns ready to fire – the only armament we carried (apart from Jimmy's rifle of course). Half an hour later three enemy planes attacked us and hit one of the other ships, a tanker, behind us. There was an inferno of noise, with bombs falling all round us. The Lascar steward grabbed Anne, Judy, and Tim and hid them under one of the dining tables whilst crockery crashed all round as we zigzagged furiously. I dashed down to our cabin to get necessities for survival in a lifeboat, a potty, blankets and first-aid box and of course the book of *Grimm's Fairy Tales*. It was strange, but I felt intensely angry, not frightened, and stuck my head out of the porthole and did 'hooky-walker' at the pilot, flying in so low that I could see his face and handlebar moustache and imagine his hand on the torpedo release mechanism. Anyway, I flattered myself that I distracted him for a second or two; the Skipper reckoned that the torpedo missed us by about six feet, and we somehow managed to sail on, only slightly damaged, for Gibraltar, which we reached five days later.

Gibraltar was an amazing and cheering sight, all brilliantly lit up after years of blackout in Malta. The children were spellbound and thought it was fairyland. All children had been evacuated from 'The Rock', so that when we took them ashore, we were surrounded by people laughing and crying who seized them from us and carried them shoulder high plying them with sweets, fruit, and old toys; reminiscent of Hamelin and the Pied Piper. We went ashore to see the Governor, Lord Gort, as we had learnt that the *Settler* was heading for the Cape, not home as we had presumed. We begged him to give us permission to tranship to be with my widowed mother, as my sister who looked after her was dying of cancer; but he refused us bluntly saying there was no ship available and anyway we were five extra mouths to feed and food was short. It was a bitter blow, and I cried my heart out for the first time in all the horror. There followed an appalling journey down the West Coast of Africa zigzagging desperately, chased much of the way by German U-boats. My husband went ashore at Lagos, West Africa, and promptly had his watch and all his money stolen. We sailed on, by now all very unfit after weeks of dreadful food, corned beef and tinned snoek, thick bread and margarine, and strong tea made with condensed milk – ugh – 5 p.m. being the last meal of the day. Finally we reached Cape Town at the end of July; the children were astonished at the abundance of food and the bright lights. On reaching our hotel I discovered we all had nits. I had to go to a chemist and ask what to do? (This got me down more than any of the horrors I had endured in Malta.) I was told to rub our heads with paraffin and put on our bathing caps for an hour and then shampoo vigorously – our heads were raw, but it did get rid of the nits. We were all pretty low physically and decided to get out of Cape Town and stay in the Marseilles Hotel by the sea at Clifton – a suburb of Cape Town.

We had had six weeks there when my husband got an order to return to Malta at the height of the blitz. I went with him to see him set sail up the east coast of Africa, leaving the children and me behind in a strange country. I was utterly desolate and would have been more so if I had known that I would not see him again until March 1943. He had apparently left Malta in November and cabled that he had seen my mother that month. My sister had died on 8 March 1942. From then on I had no news of him, except a cable to say he had been appointed Government Secretary in St Helena (he had asked to go anywhere that he could be with his family), and would come and collect us in the Cape. As the months passed with no news, I got a friend in Elgin (where I had moved with the children to a small farm cottage in the middle of a huge fruit farm), to drive me to the British High Commission in Cape Town to ask if they had any news of him, and for help as I had run out of cash. They thought he had gone down on the SS *Ceramic*, recently torpedoed off The Cape, but did not tell me. Weeks later I got a cable from Newfoundland, saying his ship was in dock for repairs; then no news until March when I got a telegram saying he was leaving the ship at Walvis Bay, the last port before Cape Town, and making his way by train. I was to meet him next day in Cape Town. His ship was torpedoed the next day. We had a couple of weeks packing up and then set sail for St Helena on board a French Cruiser, the *Indo Chinoix,* another perilous journey as the seas round The Cape were a favourite haunt of German submarines. But we arrived safely ten days later at another island, isolated but calm and peaceful after war-torn Malta.

This concludes the story of Lady Mallaby's experiences during the war. Her first husband, Jim Locker, OBE, died in India on 6 February 1951 at the age of 46, when he was the Deputy High Commissioner for the United Kingdom in Madras. She later married Sir George Mallaby, KCMG, OBE, on 2 April 1955, and on his retirement they moved to Suffolk, near Bury St

Edmunds. After his death in 1978, she moved to Blythburgh. Lady Mallaby died on 11 January 2001.

Memories of my mother, Lady Mallaby

Her son, Timothy Locker, who lives in Suffolk, adds some more detail about her long and eventful life:

In the seventeen years (1934–51) they were married, my father and mother had a most adventurous, exciting, and dramatic time; adjectives which recurred frequently throughout mother's life, not least in her early childhood. Born in Mexico City during the 1910–11 Revolution, her cot had to be moved out of the nursery on to the landing as bullets had pierced the frills through the open window.

Her father (my grandfather), Hubert Edward Brooke, was determined to fight in the Great War which had claimed the lives of many of his friends; in 1916 the family set out for England. Whilst crossing the Atlantic their ship was torpedoed; they took to the lifeboats and landed at Santander in northern Spain, the French captain of the ship refusing, not surprisingly, to go any further because of the great storms and German submarines in the Bay of Biscay. They crossed the frontier to Biarritz in the first stage of their effort to get home by land but within a few days, our mother found her father dead in bed from a heart attack; the bereaved family had to spend the rest of the war in Biarritz.

She spent the rest of her childhood and early adult years in England before, in late 1932, sailing in the *Llandudno Castle* for Cape Town, en route to her elder sister in Tanganyika (Tanzania). On board ship she met my father; they fell in love and eventually married in Dar es Salaam Cathedral on 26 May 1934. At that time my father was a young District Commissioner in a wild and remote part of northern Nyasaland (Malawi). Based on Karonga, he had absolute sway and authority over an area the size of Wales; this necessitated frequent 'Ulendos' (business safaris) to distant villages and tribes to sort out problems, etc. My mother's reminiscences describe a couple of typical incidents whilst on 'Ulendo'.

'At that time Hut Tax was 6/- (six shillings – 30p) a year, and to encourage parents not to dispose of their twins (considered an evil omen) by leaving them out in the jungle to be devoured by lions, they were exempted Hut Tax for a year if they produced their twins to be certified by the Doctor at the Boma. Once on "Ulendo", when Jimmy was holding a Barazza of the local chiefs, Corporal Julius came to my tent and said there were a lot of women wanting their twins to be certified – hearing the Bwana DC was coming they had matched up their infants accordingly so there were an inordinate number of twins.

It was on this same "Ulendo", the first with our new baby, Anne, who was being carried in a meat safe with a mattress and hinged lid to be safe from snakes and mosquitoes and carried swung on a pole by two stark naked Africans, that we stopped in a village by the name of Mweni Chinunha ('the village which smells') for Jimmy to follow up the spoor of a man-eating lion which had carried away three women and a child. In the evening I was doing my best to observe the bath-time ritual as laid down in my Baby Book; I had a small bath tub, towels, nappies, soap, and the inevitable Johnson's Baby Powder. When I took Anne out of the bath and laid her across my knees and sprinkled baby powder over her, I heard an intake of breath and long sigh and realised that all round me peering under the flaps of the tent were dozens of eyes watching my every movement – when I rubbed her with powder they thought it was flour and I was presumably going to cook her!'

[*Tim continues:*]
One way and another those two years in Nyasaland were not without incident. My father was posted back to the Colonial Office in 1937 and in that year and the following my second sister and I were born in Jersey. In April 1939 the whole family sailed for Malta (see above for my mother's story, taking us through Malta and South Africa to St Helena).

Our family remained in St Helena, Napoleon's island of exile, until April 1945 when at last we were able to return to England. After a well-earned leave, my father was posted to the Gold Coast and then in 1947 to India, where he and my mother remained pre- and post-Independence until his death. After a service in Clive of India's Fort St George, Madras, he was interred at St George's Cathedral, his grave being tended to this day.

Following our father's death in February 1951, Mother journeyed back to England to an uncertain future with three children in their early teens, very little money, and no home to go to. The facts that over the next few years she triumphantly managed, not only to keep us all at boarding school and to create an enchanting home in Wiltshire, but also managed to get married again, confirm that she was not lacking in fighting spirit, determination, and resourcefulness.

Her second marriage in 1955 to my godfather, George Mallaby, opened a glamorous and joyfully happy chapter in her life. George, a senior civil servant, was working in the Cabinet Office at the time, so they lived in a lovely terraced house off Eaton Square until George was posted in 1957 to New Zealand as UK High Commissioner. On return to England in 1960, he spent his last few years before retiring as First Civil Service Commissioner.

Widowed for the second time in 1978, my mother moved from West Suffolk to East Suffolk, where she spent the last twenty-two years of her life alone here in Blythburgh; where, particularly in the first sixteen years or so before various 'slings and arrows of outrageous fortune' beset her, she was active in many aspects of the community's life, not least in the glorious church where she spent many happy (if cold) hours at worship, flower arranging, organising a still-remembered Festival of Roses, guiding visitors or helping birds, mostly sparrows, to escape. Some further great joys for her during this period were her founding of and continuing interest in the Blythburgh Horticultural Society and, of course, the creation of her beloved garden, colourful if idiosyncratic, and also the joy and friendship she gained from the Art Group where in no time at all she would dash off the most colourful, if again idiosyncratic, paintings. She also had the joy and comfort of a wonderful circle of friends, as well as a succession of four-legged ones which gave her such fun and laughter and hair-raising adventures.

Amongst many blessings bestowed upon my mother was length of days which enabled her as the last of her generation in our wider family to experience the great joy of her ten grandchildren, eleven great grandchildren and even great-great nephews and nieces. An extensive family which reaches from England, Scotland, Wales, and Ireland, to the Channel Islands, the Falkland Islands, to North America, to Southern Africa, to Southern India, to China, Mongolia, Australia and New Zealand.

So, a life full of adventure and romance, as well as tragedy and sadness, but above all, of 'spontaneous joy and laughter, the fresh breeze of the free spirit' came to its peaceful end.

Chapter 6
A RESERVED OCCUPATION

Building Radar Stations
Richard Connick

Essential to the war effort were those in reserved occupations or engaged on essential war work. One such person was Richard (Dick) Stanley Connick, sometimes called 'Taffy'[1] He was born at Troedyrhiw South Wales on 13 November 1908 and after his marriage to Vida Flint in 1941 moved to Walberswick. Richard's main work during the war was in the construction of pylons and the laying of cables at various radar sites within the UK.

Radar, like so many inventions, was discovered quite by accident. It was in 1934 that Robert (later Sir Robert) Watson-Watt, with a team of scientists, continuing the research by Sir Edward Appleton and Dr. M. A. Barnett into reflected radio waves from various layers in the atmosphere, discovered quite by chance that they were also receiving echoes from other objects. Watson-Watt and his team therefore experimented with the detection of reflected radio waves of other distant objects and finally developed a reliable system of tracking aircraft. The system required a transmitter and a receiver built close together. The transmission pylon was built of latticework steel, 350 feet high, and the receiving pylon was 240 feet high and made of wood. Following successful trials, and with war clouds gathering, the Air Ministry decided to erect a series of detector stations all round the UK to defend the country against any possible attack from the air.

Among the contractors who were employed to erect these detector stations was Henleys, the firm Richard worked for. He relates how he came to be employed by them:

> I started work at age fourteen as a pitman in the Merthyr Vale coal mine. Life was tough in those days. I had to leave home for work at 6 a.m., walk two miles to the pit-head then a further two miles underground to get to the pit face which was under Aberfan where I

---
[1] To be a true Taffy one has to be born on the banks of the River Taff.

was working.

(Aberfan will be remembered as a place of tragic memory – in 1966 the school there was engulfed by a slag-heap killing many children and teachers.)

In 1931, after working for nine years as a collier, I decided to leave the pit and get a job with Henleys, Electrical Contractors. My eldest brother Jack was already working for them and under his tuition I became skilled in the job of linesman and pole worker. Once I was proficient in this I was sent by Henleys to work at Tiverton in Devon and at other places within the area.

Richard (right) with brother Jack on his first day at Tiverton.
(Photo from Richard Connick)

When the Air Ministry decided to build the UK-wide network of radar stations, Henleys took on some of the work and Richard was employed at a number of sites. He worked at many places in the UK including Belfast, the Isle of Man, Seaton (in Devon), Blackburn, Norwich, London, and Darsham. It was at Darsham that he had some difficulty in finding the proposed radar site of High Street, Darsham. (It was also there where he first met Vida who later became his wife):

> When my brother Ted and I were sent to Darsham we couldn't find the site where the radar station was to be built, High Street,[2] so I enquired from one of the locals where it was. This was the time when everybody had been warned not to give information to strangers in case they were spies. So when I asked this worthy if he knew and would tell me where

---

[2] The High Street Radar Station is referred to at the RAF Radar Museum Neatishead Norfolk which is well worth a visit. (At the time of writing, RAF Station, Neatishead is still in operation and is the oldest radar station in the world.)

BUILDING RADAR STATIONS

*The crew ready for work: Richard is 3rd from left.
(Photo from Richard Connick)*

this High Street in Darsham was, he just stared hard at me and ran off. He had never heard a Welsh accent before and apparently thought I was a German spy. Luckily a farmer had overheard our conversation and he recognised my Welsh accent. He also knew that there was going to be a building of sorts in High Street, Darsham and had heard that pylons were also going to be erected, so he told us where to go and all was well.

Working at heights has its dangers and there was a fatal accident while we were erecting the pylons and one man was killed but I cannot remember his name.

At one time Richard was told he was to go to the Orkneys, He was rather looking forward to this but when he was told he would be travelling by air he was not very happy and said he would rather not travel that way. They were

A RESERVED OCCUPATION

very understanding and made arrangements for somebody else to go in his place. He was sent to the Isle of Man instead, travelling by train and boat, which was much more to his liking. He was on the Isle of Man for two weeks erecting poles and laying power cables at various military and prisoner-of-war camps there.

In 1943 when he was working in Belfast and lodging in Ballymena Richard's first child, Trevor, was born. He was naturally anxious to see his newly born son and his wife Vida, so he asked his boss for a week off to visit them. For some reason his request was refused and he was bitterly disappointed. When he got back to his lodgings that evening he told his landlady what has happened. She was a very friendly and helpful individual and was highly indignant at the attitude of Richard's boss. Apparently this lady had some influence over him and told Richard not to worry, *she* would have a word with the gentleman and said, 'You ask him again'. Richard was not very hopeful but did as she had suggested. There must have been some shenanigans going on because when Richard asked again for leave he was given a letter and told to deliver it to the firm's office in Hatton Gardens, London. He duly presented himself at the office and handed in the letter. He was then told, to his surprise and joy, that his application for leave was granted and he was to report back to the office the following week. When Richard reported back they asked him to return to Ireland, but he was not very happy about this and asked if he could go somewhere else. They did and directed him to go to the Isle of Man where he had been before.

Richard's work was not confined to radar sites and he was at one time sent to work in London, repairing bomb damage. He was lodging at Plumstead at the time and had to go to Kings Cross railway station (this was when the V1 'doodle-bug' air raids had just started). He was on the train and heard a loud noise like that of a tractor engine without a silencer and, being curious, he went out and stood on the platform to see what was going on. The noise was that of a V1 flying overhead; as he watched. the engine cut out and it dived to the ground exploding with a tremendous roar. It had landed in a crowded shopping area and Richard rushed to see if he could help. However there were so many Red Cross nurses, ambulances, ARP rescue workers, police and others helping to dig people out of the rubble and attending to the wounded that he saw he could be of no assistance and left. The sight of the dead and wounded lying around horrified him and this scene has stuck vividly in his memory ever since.

Richard, like so many of those in reserved occupations or doing essential war work, had a really hard time during the war. Like those in the Armed Forces they generally had to do what they were told and couldn't change their jobs or have time off without approval. The hours were long and, after a day's work, all were expected to take part in some voluntary activities to help in the war effort. People were also enjoined to 'Dig for Victory', growing their own vegetables and fruit to help eke out the rations. Nevertheless the general health of the nation was never better.

On The Lighter Side

When Richard was working on the radar site at Darsham he lodged with a Charlie and Bessie Nunn at Lymballs Farm, Darsham. Vida Flint was a great friend of the Nunns and often came to visit them. It was on one of these visits that Richard first met Vida and was much taken with her. Bessie was a romantic and thought love might bloom between the two of them – given the right circumstances. One afternoon, therefore, she arranged for Richard to help Vida bring up the cows from the meadow. This was the first time they had been really alone together. So as they went to collect the cows Richard, who had been greatly attracted by this Suffolk beauty, asked Vida if he could start walking out with her. She agreed and on 26 December 1941 they were married and eventually went to live at 1 Norland Cottages, Walberswick.

Richard also lodged for some time at Bramfield with Don Watts, a wheelwright, and his wife Mabel. During his stay with them Dick, as they called him, had some amusing times. One day Mabel, who was going to visit a friend that afternoon, asked Dick if, in her absence, he would like to have a bath in the built-in copper, which was normally used to boil the laundry. Dick jumped at the chance, visualising a lovely long hot soak. In a country area such as Bramfield very few houses had bathrooms or hot water laid on. So to have a bath was quite a palaver. The built-in copper would be filled with water and the fire underneath lit. The hot water would then be ladled into a portable galvanised bath, usually set in front of an open fire, in another room. So the idea of having a bath sitting in the copper without all the business of carting the water from one place to another had a great attraction. Dick filled the copper, lit the fire and when the water was hot enough stripped off and leapt in with great anticipation. What he had forgotten was the fire still roaring away beneath. Dick leapt out a great deal quicker than he leapt in, running around outside in the nude until that part of his anatomy, which had received the full heat of the fire, had cooled off. 'I can tell you,' said Richard in his lilting Welsh accent, 'I never done that again'.

There was another time when Richard's brother Ted was staying with him, and because accommodation was at a premium they slept in the same room. They had gone to bed and were asleep when suddenly banging, rumblings, and knocking in the room below awoke them. They could not imagine what on earth was going on downstairs. The knocking and rumblings went on for some time but eventually all went quiet and they managed to drop off to sleep again.

In the morning, when they came downstairs for breakfast, all was revealed. Apparently Don was also the local undertaker and he had been making a coffin. It had been a rush job and being pushed for time he had built the coffin during the night. Mabel was his assistant and one of her jobs was to get into the coffins just to make sure they were strong enough.

Richard became great friends of the Watts family; and when he finally left, Mabel very kindly gave him a golden sovereign as a keepsake to remind him of his stay with them.

After the war was over Richard went to work for Blocks, Builders and Undertakers of Walberswick. In 1960 he left the building trade and worked for 6½ years in the Commissary of the United States Air Force Base at RAF Station Bentwaters. He then went back to work for Blocks until he retired in 1973.

Chapter 7

THE NURSES

A nurse and soldier's wife
Margaret Elizabeth Harwood née Fairs

Margaret was born at Manor Farm, Huntingfield, Suffolk, on 3 July 1917, coming to Walberswick in 1923 when her family moved there. Although she was christened Margaret Elizabeth her mother called her 'Margo' and she has kept that name ever since. Margo attended the Walberswick Village School and passed the scholarship examination to attend either the Lowestoft Secondary School or the Sir John Leman Grammar School at Beccles:

> I went to Lowestoft Secondary School when I was 11 years old staying as a boarder from Monday to Friday. I remember my father had to pay 12/6 – twelve shillings and six pence old money (62½ p) a week plus an occasional rabbit. I did that for a year and then went to Sir John Leman Grammar School with my brother Geoffrey[1] who was just starting there. Travelling to school was a bit different then. We cycled to the White Hart, Blythburgh, caught a bus there to Halesworth, then on by train to Beccles and then a long walk from the station to the school – it took about an hour and a half.

Margo was the first pupil to pass that examination from Walberswick Village School and the head teacher, Mrs Lee, was very proud of her achievement. Margo's was the first name recorded on the Walberswick School Honours Board and by a strange coincidence the last name recorded on that Board is that of her daughter, Margaret. (The Honours Board recorded the names of all the children who attended Walberswick School and passed this examination, referred to in later years as the 11 plus. After the school was closed the Honours Board was removed and is now on display in the Village Hall.)

After leaving school Margo became a State Registered Nurse (SRN):

> I had not really thought of nursing as a career but my mother and a friend of hers persuaded me. Because I was only 17 the Norfolk and

---

[1] See *Suffolk Memories*, pp. 5–7.

Norwich Hospital could not accept me so I went as a probationary nurse to the War Memorial Hospital in North Walsham and worked there from January 1935 to May 1937. I really loved it at North Walsham and wept when I left to go to the Norfolk and Norwich Hospital to train as an SRN. In October 1940 I took and passed my SRN finals and stayed on as a Staff Nurse, occasionally acting as Sister though I was never paid for that.

In April 1941 I married and in December of that year left the Norfolk and Norwich because of pregnancy. My daughter Margaret was born in March 1942.

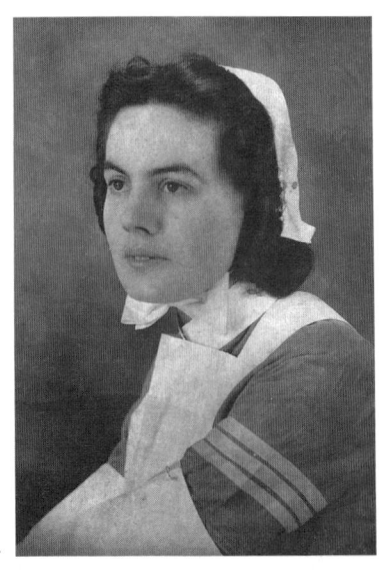

Margo in her uniform at the Norfolk and Norwich hospital. (Photo from Margo Harwood)

I had met Charles Harwood, a soldier who was stationed in Blythburgh, at a dance there and we should have been married on 29 March 1941 at 2 p.m. in Walberswick church, but Charles had to go into hospital and we were married a week later on 5 April. It seemed as if fate had taken a hand, for strangely enough on 29 March at about 1.30 p.m. a bomb was dropped on Short Lane House, a cottage not far from the church and quite close to my father's house, Ivy Cottage. [See Edith Block's story.]

The blast caused the bedroom ceiling in my father's house to fall down and the windows in the church were broken. I would have been getting ready for the wedding at the time and people would have been gathering in or near the church, so it really did seem as if a kindly fate had taken a hand in the postponement.

The Matron of the Norfolk and Norwich Hospital was one of the matrons of the old school, and she thought it was very foolish to marry in wartime. When I went back to the hospital she put me on the

The happy couple outside St Andrew's Church, Walberswick.
(Photo from Margo Harwood)

maternity block. I think she wanted to put me off getting pregnant and having to leave, which I thought was rather funny.

Whilst I was still nursing at the Norfolk and Norwich Hospital the city of Norwich experienced several visits from single bombers. The first occasion was on the afternoon of 9 July 1940. A large factory, Boulton and Paul, who made Horsa gliders, Oxford Trainer aircraft, and parts for the Hurricane, received four bombs on one of its main buildings when it was full of workmen. No air-raid alert had been sounded and there were many killed. Ninety-seven casualties were conveyed to the Norfolk and Norwich Hospital, 57 of those were serious and admitted. I remember working late into the night as I was on a surgical ward with many other nurses.

I had left the hospital when the main blitz occurred in April 1942. The hospital itself sustained serious damage in 1942, but fortunately no nurse or patient was injured. If I had not had my baby, Margaret, three weeks premature I would probably have been a patient at that time.

Baby Margaret and I stayed with Charles's parents when he first went abroad and I worked as a nurse for three days a week at a Nursing Home in Blundellsands.

After a while, at the beginning of June 1944 actually, I decided to take my daughter Margaret to visit my parents at Ivy Cottage, Walberswick. It was while I was there that my brother Geoffrey, who was in the Royal Air Force, was reported missing. Naturally my parents were very distressed, so our stay at Walberswick went on longer than I had originally planned. It was a time of waiting and hoping but, unfortunately, we had no other news about him and in time the authorities declared that he must be presumed dead. I would pass my time writing daily to Charles and waiting anxiously for letters from him.

Meantime Charles's parents had bought another house and his sister and I were offered their former house. Margaret and I returned to Crosby to make a home for Charles when, hopefully, he would return. Then in early May 1945 I received word that on 22 April my young brother Jack had been killed in Italy, so my sister Audrey, who was living in Warrington, and I returned to Walberswick to be with our parents for a time. A few days after Jack's death the war in Europe was over. It had finished just too late for Jack.[2]

After a few weeks I returned to Crosby. War in the Far East was over and I waited hopefully for Charles to return. Looking back, I would not care to go through those anxious years again.

When Charles came home in 1946 it was quite a surprise because I had no idea he was even in England. He brought home from Egypt a huge basket of various fruits, mainly citrus, none of which we had seen since before the war. It was wonderful having him home although really he was almost a stranger, since I had known him for less time than he had been abroad which was over three years.

Although ours was a whirlwind wartime marriage – meeting and marrying within eight months – we have spent many happy years together and celebrated our Diamond Wedding in April 2001, when many of the family from Walberswick attended and were able to admire the card we had received from HM the Queen.

A Naval VAD nurse

Patricia Roxburgh (née Wilson)

Patricia Roxburgh has lived in Walberswick since 1988 and takes part in many of the voluntary activities that go on in the village. She is a member of the Royal British Legion and is a Vice President of the Suffolk Branch of the British Red Cross. Her story mainly reflects the humorous side of hospital

[2] See *Suffolk Memories*, pp. 5–7.

life. To be sure, her patients were lucky to have such an attractive and delightful nurse.

War broke out whilst I was still at school. I can clearly remember being padded up in goal, playing lacrosse on the school playing field, when a lone German bomber appeared out of the sky – no warning had been given and it dive-bombed our dormitory wing. I wasn't surprised, as I always thought it looked like a barracks. Luckily there was no loss of life and it didn't do much damage though we felt a convent should not have been a target. During my latter time at school I enrolled with the Red Cross, although it was my intention to join the Royal Navy and become a Wren. However my mother and Commandant had other ideas and felt I should become a nurse. With that in mind I eventually became a Naval VAD. I passed all the required training in hospitals and was eventually sent to Kelvedon Hall, home of the Chips Channon, which was a convalescent home for the troops. Once again I narrowly missed a German missile when it passed over my head; I was returning from a few hours off-duty in Ongar. I flung the bicycle and myself into the nearest ditch. During my time at Kelvedon Hall I nursed many troops from the desert, the 8th Army. They, poor dears, were more frightened by the doodle bombs than by Rommel's Army.

Patricia in her VAD uniform.
(Photo from Patricia Roxburgh)

Besides our nursing we had to do extra fire-watching duties at night. Once I was confronted by a ghostly figure encased in plaster that slipped and fell bringing both of us down with a great crash. Luckily matron didn't hear. The same poor patient was sitting in the sun (at matron's instigation to get him outside) but it was getting too hot and I was asked to bring him in; again, with disastrous results; we both landed on the deck and he just collapsed. He was eventually sent back

Patricia with her husband Ian at the Arnhem Memorial.
(Photo from Patricia Roxburgh)

to Woolwich. A lot of patients came straight from Woolwich to avoid the bombing. One of our patients was Ben Lyon, husband of Bebe Daniels, and he soon had weekly concert parties going. There was no excuse and I shortly found myself singing and acting.

During this time my fiancé, a bomber pilot, was sadly shot down over Arnhem and reported missing. I have since located his grave and, through the kindness of the Royal British Legion, I attended with my husband Ian a wonderful memorial ceremony with the RAF colours paraded. My fiancé was shot down on the first day of MARKET GARDEN, having ordered his co-pilot and navigator to bale out, avoiding villages in Holland, for which he was posthumously honoured.

While I was still awaiting my call-up papers I was sent to Hillingdon Hall, another Convalescence Home near Harlow. From there the call came and I and another VAD, Veronica Bevan, whose uncle was the C in C, Western Approaches, were sent to HMS *Ferret*, a submarine base at Londonderry. This journey was not without its hazards, as we were held up for hours whilst a U-boat was sunk in the approaches to the Foyle outside Larne. I remember this trip very well, waving our scarlet-lined capes to the escorting destroyers.

We were very short staffed in this hospital but worked with our counterparts in St John's. This trip had its funny moments and I can safely say it was the only time I have ever socked a man under the jaw. He was a matelot trying to work his ticket and threw fits; always. I may say, when only one nurse was on duty and covering three wards. Trying to fill up a special form on these occasions and endeavouring to get a spatula into his mouth was another matter. Another patient, a Chief Petty Officer, suggested I punch him under the jaw while he held his head for me – it worked and I was able to get the spatula between his teeth to prevent him biting through his tongue. The patient was discharged.

The Navy's MO (Medical Officers) rounds took place at 8 p.m. always when only one VAD was on duty. On one occasion the chaps thought it would be fun to roll 'Tug' Wilson in a rug before the oncoming entourage appeared. Luckily they relented and released me in time to straighten myself in order to answer their required questions: 'how many DCL and SCL patients are there?'[3] and 'are the poisons etc. locked up?' I tried not to look too dishevelled and agitated. The chaps at least had the grace to give me drinks in the wardroom afterwards as compensation. They were a grand lot.

My days in Londonderry were numbered as I acquired a paralysed right arm and was invalided out in 1946. I subsequently went to a temporary Naval Hospital in London to be assessed and they decided diathermy was needed to treat my arm. I had to go to Great Portland Street Hospital to receive this treatment and used to escort a Wren with a wounded leg to the same hospital. With my arm in plaster we must have looked a funny pair as we passed Buckingham Palace and over the road, to where the police held up the Mounted Cavalry Guard for us to pass. We didn't know where to look.

Eventually I found myself at National Red Cross Headquarters acting as quartermaster to the Junior Red Cross. My right arm took two years

---

[3] Dangerous Case List and Serious Case List

to recover completely, so I had to make good use of my left and became ambidextrous. This finishes my wartime story and I thence proceeded to pastures new, ending here in Walberswick.

District and Hospital Nursing
Elsie Bally

Miss Elsie Bally's father was vicar of Needham. Her first job was nursing at the Cottage Hospital at Savernake, near Marlborough. It was her intention to become a school matron but the Matron at the Cottage Hospital was a Nightingale Nurse, having trained at St Thomas's, and she persuaded Elsie to apply to train there. She was accepted and trained from 1929 to 1933. Six months' midwifery training followed. In 1934 she applied for a post in India where she served at the Government Hospital at Patna, Bihar, from 1934 to 1938. At the end of this tour she came home and, after having helped her parents organise her sister's wedding, fully intended to take her full six months leave. However, just before Christmas 1938, she was offered a job at St Thomas's to be in charge of the district midwifery. This was too good a chance to miss and she accepted. She studied part time at the Royal College of Nursing to get her Midwife Teacher's Diploma after taking up this post.

In September 1939, when war started, the hospital maternity department was transferred to Woking. Antenatal clinics continued to be held at St Thomas's. Hospital cases were sent to Woking and those who would otherwise have had their babies at home were sent to Woking for the confinement. Antenatal clinics were held at the hospital and Elsie would go to people's houses if necessary. If labour started sooner than expected and the patient had not been evacuated, the mother would be delivered in the basement corridor of St Thomas's and then sent to Guildford, which was the hospital for emergencies. At the beginning – during the phoney war – several women got fed up and returned before their babies were delivered; and this would sometimes result in a home delivery. Elsie would be called out at all hours of the day and night. She covered by bicycle an area south of the Thames, which included Lambeth and Waterloo, sometimes distances of over two miles. They had good street maps but it was not always easy to find the streets, particularly when having to contend with heavy traffic. It was easy to find herself in the midst of it and unable to turn. At night with blackout conditions it was particularly hazardous. All the lights on vehicles, including bicycles, were half obscured and she was dressed in navy blue uniform.

She particularly remembers one Sunday morning when she was making a routine visit to a woman who had had her baby. The radio was on and the husband wanted to stay in the room to listen to an important announcement that was to be made. This must have been the Prime Minster, Neville Chamberlain, declaring war on Germany.

The nurses all had rooms in the Nurses' Home over the road. It was called Riddell House and Lord Riddell of the *News of the World*, whose wife had been a Nightingale Nurse, had had it built. This was very modern and comfortable and the nurses would keep their belongings in their rooms but, because of the bombing, they slept in the semi-basement of the hospital.

During the phoney war, the Operating Theatre for general patients was also transferred to Woking. There was a shortage of theatre staff there and Matron asked Elsie to go to help out as she had done quite a bit of theatre work before the war. She was there for about a fortnight, during which time they dealt with a lot of casualties from Dunkirk. The theatre was working non-stop for 48 hours cleaning up and dressing these casualties. The first blitz happened when she was in Woking and she asked to go back to London; one of her midwives had been killed in that raid and she felt she was needed there.

St Thomas's was bombed several times and the main thing Elsie remembers is the dust and dirt. Early on the windows were blown out and they had to contend with splintered glass on the floors. After this, because of the danger of getting broken glass into their shoes which they kept beside their beds at night, the nurses slept with their shoes under their pillows. Elsie was District Sister and the nurses who worked on the district were well used to being called out at all times of the day and night. Not only did they sleep with their shoes under the pillow but their clothes as well. However, it was easier when the glass was replaced by cardboard as when that was blown out they could easily put it back and there was no more broken glass.

There was always the fear that the bombing would breach the Thames embankment and cause the hospital to flood. She remembers some flooding in the basement once, and having to slosh through the water. Her main memory is the mess which generally followed a raid. The morning after a blitz everything was filthy.

They ran an infant welfare clinic in the hospital and at Christmas a party would be held for the children in the basement. The nurses made golliwogs and other toys for them.

By the time of the doodlebugs Elsie had become Superintendent of District Nurses in Essex. She had an office in County Hall at Chelmsford. She was also responsible for overseeing nursing homes and the training of District Nurses. She covered quite a large part of Essex. After that, and still during the war, she moved to Boston, Lincolnshire, as Chief Nursing Officer for one of the three county areas, where she remained until her retirement to Walberswick in 1963. Here she built St Francis, a house in Seven Acre Lane and created her large and beautiful garden. In 1994 she moved to Oaklands, a retirement home in Reydon, where she has a small garden which she enjoys tending herself.

Elsie does not enjoy the best of health but is comfortably settled in the pleasant surroundings of Oaklands and is always pleased when visited by her family and friends, especially those from Walberswick.

Chapter 8
WIVES AND MOTHERS

A near miss: when a bomb demolished Short Lane Cottage
Edith Block née Glasspool

Edith Block has lived in Marlish, a semi-detached house nearly opposite St Andrews Church, all her married life. She was born at Boxgrove, Sussex, in 1909 as Edith Glasspool. She first came to Walberswick when she worked for the Davis family as nanny to their children. The Davises had built a house here to use as a holiday home; they subsequently moved here permanently and Edith intended to wait until the Davis family was settled before finding another job in London.

I joined the Walberswick Badminton Club. It was there that I met Leighton Block and this changed my whole life. We fell in love and on

From left to right: Olive Quenzer, Edith Block, Bill Quenzer, Wally Merton, and Leighton Block.
(Photo from Edith Block)

*Marlish in the course of construction.
(Photo from Edith Block)*

7 August 1937 we were married at Boxgrove Priory Church, and after our honeymoon settled permanently in Walberswick.

Before we married I had become great friends with Leighton's sister Olive and her husband Bill Quenzer, and in 1936, after Leighton and I became engaged, the four of us bought a piece of land with the idea of building ourselves a pair of semi-detached houses. After a great deal of scrimping and saving and giving up of spare time and with the help of Leighton's brothers, Henry and Eddy, Marlish and Benrite were built. Olive and Bill moved into their new home in April 1937 and Leighton and I followed after our honeymoon.

When war broke out in 1939 Leighton, who was a carpenter in the family business of Block, Builders and Exors, was placed on the Reserved Occupation list. He was employed throughout the war in building pillboxes, blockhouses, airfields, repairing bomb damage and

A NEAR MISS: WHEN A BOMB DEMOLISHED SHORT LANE COTTAGE

doing other works essential to the war effort, including the building of minesweepers at the Lowestoft shipyard.

Shortly after war broke out the population of the village was increased enormously by the arrival of the military with all their equipment. After the fall of France and the Lowlands there was always the danger of invasion by sea or air and subsequently Walberswick and the area around it was used for defence and training. The heathland adjacent to Hoist Wood was used for live firing and grenade practice and a searchlight battery with a Nissen hut was built on Squires Hill. Blockhouses were built on the fields overlooking the beach and there was an anti-tank roadblock in the main street near to what was known as 'The Towers'. The normal activities of the village and its residents were often disrupted and individuals 'put about', especially during military exercises. Edith relates:

> On 29 June 1940 I gave birth to Timothy, my eldest son, and three days later, on the 2nd July I was ordered to leave home, albeit temporarily,

The happy wedding group outside Boxgrove Priory Church, showing Leighton's brother Henry in the back row, 2nd left.
(Photo from Edith Block)

161

by the military. They warned me that there would be artillery firing their guns over our house and, because some rounds might just drop short, I was to move out of my home for the duration of the exercise. My sister-in-law, Olive Quenzer, who lived in the other half of the semi-detached house (Benrite) with her 14-month-old daughter Mary, was also ordered to leave. An ambulance came to move my baby and me to Poplar Cottage, a house on the village green and the home of Leighton's eldest brother, Henry. Here we spent the day until the artillery had stopped firing and the exercise was over. We became used to incidents such as these and regarded them as just an annoying inconvenience.

The following year though we were faced with a dangerous situation when our part of the village became the target of a German Luftwaffe bomber.

It was in March 1941. I had been busy all morning with my household chores and had prepared a meal for nine-month-old Timothy who was asleep in his pram outside in the garden. At about one o'clock the air-raid siren suddenly sounded and, at that time, this was unusual during daylight hours. I heard anti-aircraft guns firing in the distance so thought that, just in case, I had better get the pram closer to the house. I had just begun to move it when I heard the roar of an aircraft coming in very low and clearly saw the dreaded swastika on the fuselage. As the aeroplane zoomed overhead fountains of earth shot upwards and I thought the plane must have hit something. In fact it had dropped a bomb at the bottom of the garden. I had just got to the door of the house when there was a loud bang as the bomb exploded. The plaster ceiling in the house came down, windows blew out along with the curtains and the sideboard doors flew open smashing and scattering all the china. There was dirt, dust and debris everywhere. Almost immediately a second bomb was dropped and this landed on Short Lane Cottage only a short distance away. I was in a daze and held on to the door of the house, and poor Timothy was crying with fright. There was no sign of the meal I had prepared for him; it must have been blown to smithereens by the blast from the explosion. Strangely I remember being not so much frightened as angry about it all because the blast had killed the few chickens we had kept to supplement our rations and after all the poor chickens had done nobody any harm. A piece from one of the bombs had also made a hole right through the

A NEAR MISS: WHEN A BOMB DEMOLISHED SHORT LANE COTTAGE

Timothy in the pram in which he was so nearly killed.
(Photo from Edith Block)

walls of the living room where we would normally have been sitting. There was nothing I could do because everything was covered in dust and filth. Somewhere I found a cover, gave it a good shaking, wrapped it around Timothy and dashed next door to see if my sister-in-law Olive was all right.

Olive's house was in the same state as mine but, in her case, the door was also down. Living with Olive and her toddler Mary was my elderly mother-in-law granny Block and she thought the bomb had actually hit the house.

I was desperate and felt confused, Timothy's head was covered with scratches, but my main concern was about his feed, which had disappeared. What on earth was I to do to replace it?

Olive went to gather her little girl Mary from upstairs in the bedroom. This was a hazardous operation because the electric wiring was hanging down all over the place and Olive was afraid she might be electrocuted. With some difficulty she managed to evade the danger and together, we all scrambled out of the house.

We ran up the adjacent field to Ryecroft, where a Mrs Gilbert lived who was a friend. I was still concerned about Timothy's midday meal and to my relief Mrs Gilbert kindly provided the means at last to give Timothy his feed.

The local doctor had been notified about what had happened and he came to examine Timothy. He said that, luckily, he was all right except for the scratches on his head and they were only superficial. But he told Edith that if she had not brought Timothy into the house when she did, the blast and flying glass would have killed him.

Edith was so shocked that she dared not return to her house and stayed with Mrs Gilbert at Ryecroft. She was despondent, thinking that after only three years, this was the end of the home she and Leighton had worked and struggled so hard to make.

A short time after the bombing one of the Air Raid Wardens, Bill Winyard, came dashing up to see if there were any casualties, what damage had been done and if he could be of any assistance. Edith asked if he could possibly get a message to Leighton who was working about four or five miles away near Wenhaston, engaged in building pillboxes. Bill Winyard got word to Leighton through the Wenhaston Post Office telling him that a bomb had damaged his house but that Edith and baby Timothy were all right. Leighton immediately left work and cycled home to Walberswick as fast as he could. When he got home there was no sign of Edith and the baby, only a lone soldier who been posted to guard the damaged properties. After anxiously looking around Leighton finally found Edith at Ryecroft. He went back to the house, gathered up all their clothes, collected Edith and the baby and went to Poplar Cottage again where his brother Henry made him welcome. (Olive, with toddler Mary, stayed with Ellen (Bubby) Stannard in Lorne Cottages at the top of the village green.) That evening Edith had an attack of delayed shock; the blood drained from her face and she began to

A NEAR MISS: WHEN A BOMB DEMOLISHED SHORT LANE COTTAGE

tremble uncontrollably. After a time, as Leighton and the others comforted and consoled her, the attack passed and she spent a reasonable night.

Edith and Leighton stayed at Poplar Cottage for four weeks whilst light emergency repair work was being done to the house. The kitchen window was replaced and the others boarded up. They then returned to live in their still-damaged home. A Morrison shelter was put in the living room and, because the damage upstairs was so bad and the first floor not safe to use, they had to live and sleep downstairs. It was not until the late 40s or early 50s that their house was finally and completely repaired.

Short Lane Cottage, where the second bomb had been dropped, was quite close to Edith's house. A Mrs Taylor lived there and she was at home at the time. Miraculously she climbed out over the rubble in a very bad state of shock but otherwise unhurt. The house was almost completely demolished and it was many years before it was rebuilt.

Edith's second son, Andrew, was born in December 1944 and all he could see from his window was the remains of the bombed house. It made such an impression on him that when he went to school he made a linocut of the view. For many years he, Timothy, and other boys would use the house and bomb crater as a place to play.

Edith tells of another rather frightening experience. It happened in March 1944:

> I was walking over to Southwold via the military Bailey Bridge with Timothy and sister-in-law Olive and her second daughter Judy. The air was full of the sound of the drone and throbbing of aircraft. As we looked we saw in the direction of Henham a massive formation of American bombers circling and forming up with their protective fighters. We were marvelling at the sight of these great planes getting into formation when suddenly it appeared that one of the fighters tipped the wing of a bomber and it began to fall. As it did so it collided with another bomber and they both fell to the ground over Henham woods. As the planes hit the ground a huge pall of smoke formed and we waited for the sound to hit our ears of the explosion that must follow this awful crash. The other bombers just continued their circling and formation. It all seemed very odd to us that, although we had witnessed this dreadful crash and many others must have seen or heard it, nothing was ever reported in the press of the incident.

WIVES AND MOTHERS

The following story, kindly given by Richard Pymar, a member of the Halesworth (Holton) Air Field Memorial Association, is believed to explain what Edith and Olive actually saw:

On the 29th March 1944 a force of seventy-seven B24 Liberator Heavy Bombers, carrying heavy armour-piercing bombs, assembled over Henham near Blythburgh for an intended raid on a German V weapons site at Watten and the submarine pens at St Nazaire, France.

The force was from the USAAF 20th Combat Wing made up of approximately thirty planes from the 93rd Bomb Group base at Hardwick and the rest from the 446th Bomb Group based at Bungay and 448th Bomb Group from Seething.

What happened next is not too clear but at about 1045 hours one of the 93rd Bomb Group fell out of formation and collided with another of the same Group cutting the fuselage of the latter aircraft in two. Almost immediately wreckage began to fall on Lord Stradbroke's estate at Henham. Both aircraft were carrying a full bomb load. The fuselage of the second Liberator fell into trees near the A145 (Beccles road). Henham Hall was severely damaged as bombs exploded in the vicinity.

The emergency services were quickly on the scene; many of the rescuers came from Halesworth airfield, the home of the 56th Fighter Group. An ambulance and the National Fire Service from Southwold were also there.

At about 1130 hours, whilst a search was being carried out near the main crash site, an enormous explosion occurred within the wreckage. It is believed that at least 19 United States Army Air Force (USAAF) personnel were killed and a further 38 injured. One of the dead Americans was a brilliant fighter pilot from Halesworth, Captain Stanley Morrill.

Out of the twenty airmen who made up the crew of the two Liberators, three miraculously survived. If you visit the site of the crash today the scarring on the trees can still be seen and pieces of debris found from the aircraft.

In 1994 a memorial was erected in Henham Park by the 6th Earl of Stradbroke and dedicated to the two crashed Liberators and their crews.

To get back to Edith's story:

> The grounds of the two semi-detached houses, Marlish and Benrite, were a fair size and, about the time the war started, a proper dugout shelter had been built. This was used for our two families, including granny Block and for Leighton's middle brother Eddie and his family who had a house just behind. Since the bombing, however, in which Eddie's house was also damaged, Eddie and his family had moved and no longer used the dugout shelter. One night after this at about 10 p.m. the air-raid siren sounded and the two families went to the shelter. It was not long before the sound of explosions and machine gun fire was heard. We looked up into the night sky and saw tracer bullets flying overhead. The noise was terrific and we all thought the village was getting a real pasting. Eventually things quietened down and the 'All Clear' went. By this time it was very late and as we were all quite comfortable in the shelter we decided to stay there until morning. The intensity and noise of the firing had been so fierce that we all expected to see most of Walberswick flattened, but miraculously the village was untouched. All the firing, explosions, and noise had been made by our own troops who had been having a military exercise during the night. Not for the first time the military had forgotten to inform us what was going to happen. Like many other villagers, we were not very amused, but by this time we had become used to being 'inconvenienced'.

So ends Edith's story of her wartime memories. Compared with those days Walberswick is quiet but it will never be the same peaceful place it was before the war. Its popularity as an area of outstanding natural beauty means an invasion of another kind but as Edith says, 'The invasion of visitors and their traffic is a small price to pay for living in such a lovely village.'

Home and Duty
Vida Connick née Flint

Vida Christine Flint was born at Hill Farm, Westhall, on 17 July 1921. She first came to Walberswick in 1938 and continued to work and made her home there during the war.

On Boxing Day 1941 she married Richard Connick and went to live at 1 Norland Cottages, Walberswick. They had three children, two born during the war, Trevor in 1943 and Ann in 1944 (Rita was born in 1951). Both wartime babies were born in the maternity ward at the Patrick Stead Hospital, Halesworth.

During the later stages of her pregnancy with her second child Ann, Vida, who had her mother staying with her, decided to go to Southwold to do some shopping. They went over on the ferry, just a rowing boat. (The steam chain ferry, the Blyth, had been put out of action during the invasion scare in 1940, and was moored in a sunken position in midstream.) It was 9 November and a wild day so they had a bit of a rough ride in the boat. Vida suddenly started to have the pangs of labour. She was not due until 30 November and her first confinement with Trevor took two days so she did not worry and thought there was no need to go to the hospital yet. Anyway, things had quietened down and she didn't want to leave baby Trevor until the last moment. Next day however, in the middle of an air raid with doodlebug's (V1s) flying overhead she started labour in earnest and had to get to the hospital in a hurry. She called her friend Ellen Stannard, a qualified Red Cross Nurse, who confirmed the urgency of the situation and arranged for a taxi to take them both to the Patrick Stead Hospital, Halesworth. In less then half an hour after arriving baby Ann was born. To use a famous phrase, it was 'a close run thing'.

Vida and Richard.
(Photo from Vida Connick)

During the war the baby clinic was held in Wenhaston, some five miles away, and Vida would walk there from Walberswick with her two babies in a pushchair to collect bottles of orange juice and cod liver oil. The Ministry of Food provided these for all babies and young children to boost their

Vida with Trevor and Ann ready for a jaunt on her bicycle.

(Photo from Vida Connick)

vitamin intake. These and National Dried Milk which was also available would be delivered to the village if required, probably by the district nurse or a member of the WVS. Vida, however, preferred to walk the five miles to Wenhaston; as she said, 'It was good for the babies to be in the fresh air and the exercise was good for me'.

When Richard was working in the west of the country he would sometimes visit his parents in South Wales and Vida, with her two babies, would get on a train to meet him and stay there with him. She loved travelling but during wartime the trains would be packed, mostly with military personnel and all their gear, making it very difficult, but Vida's adventurous spirit overcame them all.

WIVES AND MOTHERS

At one time Vida had her two brothers John and Leonard visiting her at 1 Norland Cottage and the air raid siren sounded and enemy aircraft started bombing Southwold. Vida grabbed her children and got under the heavy table in the living room for shelter – the wise and proper thing to do. Her brothers however dashed outside to see what was going on – a foolish thing to do, for there was always the likelihood that a stray bomb might be dropped close by and there was a very real chance of being hit by shrapnel from exploding shells of the anti-aircraft guns.

Vida talked about the soldiers who were stationed in Walberswick. They would practise their drill on the village green and the children loved to watch them. When the Cameronians were stationed in Walberswick the children, and Vida, were particularly fascinated by the kilts they wore and the bagpipes they played.

There was a NAAFI Canteen in what is now the Parish Lantern where the military could get refreshments and buy cigarettes, toiletries, and various other necessities. There was also the 'Wave Crest' café down by the river which was owned and run by Vida's uncle Mr ('Hoody') Spall and his cousin Miss Isobel Norman. The soldiers were particularly fond of the home-cooked fare offered, especially Miss Norman's famous Suffolk rusks. Sadly 'Wave Crest' is no more as it was washed away during the 1953 floods.

Vida remembers how very happy everyone was during the Victory Day celebrations. A huge bonfire was lit on the salt flats by the river. A piano had been put on top of a lorry and somebody was playing it to provide the music. Everyone in the village was there and they all joined hands dancing around and singing the songs that had been popular during the war. It was a wonderful night.

Richard and Vida thank God that they and their family got safely through the War and now, in the eventide of their lives, enjoy the peace and quiet of Walberswick.

Chapter 9
CARE OF CHILDREN

Barnardo Children
Mary Joy Sanger

Mrs Mary Joy Sanger (née Sparkes) first came to Walberswick in 1934 to visit her aunt, Mrs Stapley, who owned 'Seagulls' in Stocks Lane. She came several times with her fiancé, a medical student, and in 1939 they were married and spent their honeymoon on a farm near Helston in Cornwall. The area was even then preparing for war and the farmland round Culdrose was taken over for an air station.

By then her husband had qualified and was a surgeon working in the Southern group of hospitals and they lived at Rochford, Essex. Upon the outbreak of war he became part of an emergency team of doctors based at Runwell in what had been a large mental hospital. These emergency teams were set up at various points near the East Coast in case of invasion. It was not long after this he joined the RAF and worked in various RAF hospitals, mostly in this country, throughout the war, rising to the rank of Wing Commander.

Joy went home to her mother in Surrey and looked for some war work. Having no qualifications and loving children, she volunteered to work at a Dr Barnardo Home for children under the age of five at Merstham near Reigate. There were 35 children at the home and they came from the East End of London. Some were orphans and others had parents who were unable to take care of them. The home was a run-down old Victorian house, ill equipped to take young children. None of the assistants was trained, but they worked night and day nursing the children through all sorts of childish ailments.

The Battle of Britain took place over that area and barrage balloons were all around. They were subjected to a great deal of bombing. No proper shelters had been built in the house or the grounds; there were cellars but they were too damp to be used for this purpose and Joy remembers having to put the children to bed in their bunks and hoping for the best.

Joy continued to live at her own home, returning every evening unless she happened to be on night duty. She was paid the handsome sum of sixteen shillings (80p) per week. The staff did all the washing and ironing by hand: there was no such modern equipment as washing machines, dryers, or rotary irons.

During the hot weather the children were allowed to run in the garden without their clothes on and for fun they would have the hose turned on them. The children loved this but the neighbours complained, saying it was indecent. They solved that problem by begging bits of wool from all their friends and knitting little garments for them. The children had no toys and tended to be mischievous because they were so bored. There was a kindergarten close by, so Joy went there to find out all about the playgroup they used to run there. She then organised a playgroup and a little school at the home. On Joy's half days she would sometimes take four of them for a ride on the top of a bus just for a treat.

There was a Canadian Army [Commando] camp opposite in the grounds of Jeremiah (Mustard) Coleman's house and the soldiers would come over and help with the children. They would help to bath them and brought them beautiful presents at Christmas.

The children would sometimes be taken into the grounds opposite and have a picnic with the Canadian soldiers. They crossed the road in a line, each hanging onto the clothes of the child in front, while the Canadians held up the traffic. One day they came over and said, 'We won't be seeing you tomorrow'. It transpired that they had gone on a raid [Dieppe?] and sadly most of them didn't come back.

The children stayed at the home until they were five years old and were then taken to Headquarters in London; from there they would be sent to other homes. Joy remembers one little boy clinging to her. He is now sixty, a successful writer, and still visits her here in Walberswick.

There was one matron in the Home who was very strict and sometimes cruel; she would shut the children in cupboards if they misbehaved, but she had three favourite children whom she allowed into her room. One day she went out, leaving Joy and one other assistant in charge. One of the head officials of Barnardo's, a Mr Kirkpatrick, came round to make a visit. He happened to see two of these children who appeared to be drunk. The other girl was quite all right and wanted to hide them, but Joy said they should let Mr Kirkpatrick know what had happened. It transpired that the children had taken some of the Matron's sleeping pills and they were pretty nearly dead.

An ambulance was called and they were rushed to hospital to be treated; fortunately they survived. That matron was dismissed; another was appointed in her place who was a wonderful person with the children.

In spite of the bombing and the responsibility of looking after the children, Joy looks back on some very happy times she had during the war at this Barnardo's Home.

Children from concentration camps
Jean Pappworth

Mrs Jean Pappworth first came to Walberswick on holiday in the late 1950s with her three daughters. They stayed at 'Westwood' where Mea Allen and Grace Woodbridge ran a B&B. Later on, she and the children with a friend and her children rented and shared 'Crows Nest', spending their summer holidays there. Many years later, Anna Freud, who knew how much Jean loved Walberswick, told her of a house that was about to be sold. She was offered first refusal of 'Seagulls' which she happily accepted.

Jean was born in Hampstead, London, in 1923. She first went to St Margaret's School, then the King Alfred Progressive School, and finally to a school in Switzerland.

On the outbreak of war she returned to England and, at age sixteen, joined the Women's Land Army in Warwickshire, working for a short time as a Land Girl where she spent most of her time planting cabbages in the fields. She subsequently returned to London and joined the Red Cross as a VAD nurse. She was sent to the Royal Masonic Hospital, Hammersmith, to do basic nursing and was then posted to a soldiers' convalescent home at Windsor.

*The Land Girl.
(Photo from Jean Pappworth)*

CARE OF CHILDREN

Jean was then sent to the Blood Transfusion Centre at Slough, where the doctor in charge was the haematologist Janet Vaughan. She then returned to London and lived with her parents in a block of flats in the West End. This was the time when London was being bombed by the V1s. They would hear the V1s come over, mainly at night, and when the engine stopped would wait with bated breath for the ensuing thud and explosion, wondering where it had landed. At first, whenever the air-raid warning was sounded, they would dutifully traipse down to the shelter but gradually, like most people, Jean and her parents became blasé and didn't bother. Fortunately Jean and her parents survived the whole war physically unscathed: the only damage done to their flat was having the windows blown out once.

Jean in her Red Cross uniform with patients. (Photo from Jean Pappworth)

Jean worked at two different wartime day nurseries which had been set up to take care of children whose mothers were doing essential war work. She would cycle the five miles from her home to the nursery and would take it in turns with her companion nursery workers to arrive at 7.30 a.m. to open up the nursery in time to receive the working mothers' children before they went off to do their war work.

CHILDREN FROM CONCENTRATION CAMPS

Right at the end of the war Jean volunteered to work at a Reception Centre, set up in an ex-Army camp near Windermere, for children from the Therezienstadt Concentration Camp. The Centre was run by the Central British Fund (CBF) for Jewish Refugees.[1] Many of her fellow volunteers were refugees from the Nazis themselves and not a lot older than the boys that they were going to help to rehabilitate. They all travelled by train together, to the Lake District getting to know one another during the journey.

There was a short time to spare before the children were due to arrive, and it was spent preparing the accommodation, trying to make the army huts as 'home-like' as possible and each volunteer was assigned to what appeared to be the most appropriate job. Jean was asked to paint a series of large panels to decorate the dining hall.

On arrival the children were separated into two groups. By far the largest was that of boys of about 15 years plus, mostly from Poland, Czechoslovakia, and Germany. They were cared for under the supervision of a man who had come to England as a refugee himself, having spent time as an enemy alien on the Isle of Man.

The smaller group, of younger children, was under the supervision of a woman with a similar background. All of these children were orphans. It was to this younger group that Jean was assigned. Boys and girls aged about 4–6 years. Each helper was allotted three or four children to be in her special care, the object being to try to replicate a 'family' situation as closely as possible.

One of the problems was communication as the children spoke no English and Jean spoke no German. There came an opportunity to use this to help build a relationship with one little girl who was a great joker. At bath-time Jean asked her to teach her some German. With a serious face the child pointed to her nose saying '*das ist pferd*' [horse], to her mouth '*und das ist hund*' [dog] and so on taking great pleasure in fooling Jean into learning wrong words.

This making of a relationship was an important objective, as closeness and trust with an adult was what these children had not known since separating from their parents.

---

[1] The television programme shown on Channel 4 (8 p.m., 28 September 2000), 'The Children who escaped from the Nazis', refers to this organisation.

CARE OF CHILDREN

At first bread was saved by the children from meals and hidden, in order to be sure there was food in reserve, as had been necessary in the Camp.

It was a beautiful autumn, in a beautiful part of England, and one of the pleasures was taking the children for walks in the countryside. This, too, was a novel experience for these children. There was one little boy in Jean's group of whom she was especially fond who expressed his appreciation with great feeling, '*Oh ist so schöne.*' [Oh it is so beautiful.]

Subsequently the children were moved. The older boys went to various hostels in different parts of the country, where they were offered training to equip them for earning a living.

The younger children went as a group to a house in Surrey, which had been donated for the purpose. There the 'family' feeling was reinforced and they did in fact make great efforts to maintain strong links with each other for the remainder of their lives, although later they scattered; some were adopted, some remained in England, others going to Israel, America, Australia, and Italy. They continue to have reunions from time to time at different venues and make great efforts to attend such occasions.

The woman initially in charge in Windermere was much loved by them all; she became a mother-figure for them, and when she appeared as the central figure in 'This is your Life' on television, many came from all over the world to celebrate with her.

Chapter 10
SCHOOL CHILDREN

Childhood memories of my life in World War II
Margot Godbold

Margot Godbold first came to Walberswick from Hindhead in 1987:
> I had fallen under its spell on a brief visit earlier in that decade. I had always loved East Anglia and when my mother died in 1987 I decided to buy a house in Walberswick for all the family to enjoy – after all my husband was born only 10 miles away in Wissett. We'd be back where we belonged.
>
> I am an only child and in 1939 was living in North London and being educated at our local convent, the Marie Auxiliatrice, known as Manor House school. In 1939 during the 'phoney war', my school had been evacuated to a large house in Marnhull in Dorset which had been extremely primitive. The experience had galvanised the nuns into seeking better accommodation for their school should hostilities break out in earnest. At the outbreak of war therefore, they were well prepared and as many parents as wished were invited to send their children to a beautiful house in the Cotswold village of Rodmarton. I was eager to join the exodus from London. The school stories I devoured had filled me with joyful expectation – midnight feasts, jolly japes and the joys of being 'a boarder' – something to which I had long aspired.
>
> The journey down by coach with my suitcase and my overly large packet of egg sandwiches was on a gloriously sunny September day. Our arrival remains somewhat blurred in my memory except for the immediate worry on my part of the loss of my remaining egg sandwiches, which far exceeded any thoughts of homesickness or fury at being put in the 'babies' dormitory'.
>
> Cotswold winters can be bitter and that winter was exceedingly cold. I remember watching my music teacher being pulled from the village, where the lay staff was billeted, on a sledge by her companions – and

SCHOOL CHILDREN

*Part of the garden at Rodmarton – the pond in which I fell is at the end of the path.
(Photo from Margot Godbold)*

she was no lightweight. I remember sledding down the hills on the compulsory walks we all had to make at the weekends. I also remember my best friend's fingers being swollen and sore with chilblains and trying to keep warm around the huge fire that had been lit in the ballroom.

About a hundred of us had gone to Rodmarton, probably about two-thirds of the school. The mansion had its own private chapel, which was served by the monks of Prinknash Abbey – essential, I imagine, for the spiritual well-being of the nuns. We had at least three classes in the main part of the ballroom – which had two beautiful, very modern pale oak grand pianos at one end – and small groups in the three alcoves. There were two classes in the library and possibly a smaller class of the oldest girls elsewhere. During that first winter I started learning to play the piano and had as my practice instruments such diverse keyboards as dulcitones, minitones, upright pianos and grand pianos. I joined the 'Band' and made music with anything that came to hand. I learned to dance the waltz and the foxtrot in the ballroom at the weekends to a wind-up gramophone. We kept ourselves amused with games of monopoly on a German monopoly board owned by Else who had been in my class since before the war. We never questioned why she was there or bothered at all about buying hotels on the Unter den Linden. I vividly remember bruising the inside of my knees purple by pogo-sticking up and down the long corridor outside the ballroom and library. We must have wreaked untold damage to the beautiful pale wooden floor and rugs that lay along it, as we were stopped from this pastime afterwards.

As the winter receded and thoughts were turning to producing enough food for everyone in the country we were given tasks in the garden and the fields in lieu of homework. Two of these that I recall were picking the caterpillars off the cabbages and picking the flowers off the potato plants as it was thought at the time to stimulate a better crop of potatoes. We had a wonderful head gardener who, I learnt later from an article in the RHS magazine, was held in great esteem in the gardening world. William Scruby was only just literate, but he had made a garden that, even as a child, I could appreciate as being something special. There were exotic plants in greenhouses, wonderful massed borders, and ponds with newts in – I fell in twice attempting to catch newts – and grottoes and hidey-holes that children love to play in.

As spring went into summer and the weather remained hot and sunny day after day, our classrooms went into the garden. Every day we would take our tables and chairs out to our chosen spot and have our lessons under the shade of trees. This was the first time I became aware of loopers – those little caterpillars that love hanging from silver birch trees and drop unerringly down your neck.

My school was extremely keen on games and gym and we were drilled for our Sports Day for what seemed weeks beforehand. That summer was no different and when the day dawned bright and sunny and parents began arriving, the first strains began to make themselves apparent. Girls looking pale would disappear. The older ones looked distinctly green. But the show went on. It gradually became obvious; however, that the numbers taking part were diminishing rapidly and by the end of the afternoon the nuns were inside dealing with a massive outbreak of sickness and diarrhoea. I can just remember the scenes of

SCHOOL CHILDREN

chaos with nuns and parents running hither and thither with bowls and cloths. I was one of the few lucky ones who escaped.

The summer of 1940 was considered very unsafe in London so my mother came down and stayed in the village for the summer holidays. Those of us who remained in school helped in the fields getting in the harvest. My ankles got very sore from the stubble and I got bitten by harvest bugs but I loved it. I had learned to ride a bicycle that summer, riding on the pedals of a 28-inch bike, and my mother bought me one more my size in Cirencester. After that we went off on cycle rides together and it seemed an idyllic time.

That autumn the news from the war front was not good and things were getting difficult for us, too. I think, looking back, it must have been quite a problem feeding us and maybe getting staff to teach us. A number of the lay staff had left and I don't remember new ones replacing them. We had two visitors, however, firstly Queen Mary and then the Emperor Haile Selassie, who made a great impression on me. Not for what they said, but because, being one of the smallest in the school, I and five others of like size, were made to sit on large velvet cushions of brilliant hue at the front of the school more comfortably seated on chairs. We had strict instructions not to move. Both Queen Mary and the Emperor looked exactly as they appeared in their pictures – very upright, very grand, and quite intimidating to a small girl. The reason for their visits I never knew. I only knew that it was considered a great honour and that they came from the big house at Badminton where, I understand, both had been staying at various times.

We also, from time to time, had visits from the Abbot of Prinknash Abbey and that was a real treat. He was most approachable and fun and, if he was staying, we all vied to take him his meal – taking meals to the resident monk was one of our tasks.

During this time the bombing raids were at their height and if the planes were on their way to bomb Coventry they passed over us and the sirens would sound. We would have to put on our dressing gowns and slippers and take our eiderdowns and go down to the cellars and wait for the all clear. This was a most uncomfortable experience, crouched together on wooden benches for what seemed like hours at a time.

CHILDHOOD MEMORIES OF MY LIFE IN WORLD WAR II

We were always aware of the war although we never listened to the radio. Two of our nuns were French and one of my favourites affected me greatly when she wept openly at the fall of Paris. The other one had the habit of calling us 'Little Hitlers' if we dared show torchlight after lights out. I evolved a system of reading by crawling down to the bottom of the bed and then putting my torch on. Two bombs did in fact fall near us a few fields away and we had an expedition to see the craters – luckily they did no damage. Bombers returning from the Midlands were thought to have dropped their remaining load before crossing the Channel. About this time I can remember we had a visit from one of our 'old girls'. She had been School Captain and was quite a heroine of mine. She arrived dressed from head to toe in leathers and on her despatch rider's motorbike – an impressive sight. I longed to emulate her but the only thing open to me was to knit the endless pullovers, socks, and balaclava helmets that were wanted by our troops. The colour was off-putting, the sizes were vast, I was a very slow knitter and house points were involved. The crunch came when someone took one of my knitting needles when I was on the point of finishing my allotted sleeve. I was desperate, searching everywhere and asking everyone for a spare needle. No joy. The only solution I could think of was to take someone else's. I shall never forget the outcry. The scorch of condemnation lives with me still. The trouble was that everyone knew that I had lost my knitting needle – the culprit was easy to find.

I was quite ill that winter. We had to walk to the village hall for our indoor games and gym lessons and by the time I had walked there I had crippling stomach pains and had to sit through the session. The same thing happened after the walk back, but it was some time before any notice was taken of my problem. Eventually I was put to bed and given codeine and quinine to stop the pain and take my temperature down. I was also fed platefuls of prunes as the nuns thought constipation might be the problem. Luckily, I had friends who came to see me and ate all the prunes. Some three years later I had acute appendicitis and looking back on the earlier incident I think my appendix was probably grumbling painfully then. The doctor was never called and after a week's rest in bed I went back to school. I don't think my parents ever knew until I told them in the holidays. I also had chicken pox and so did everybody else. One after the another we went down with it and were put in the 'chicken run'. We weren't allowed to lie and do nothing, however. It was exam time and we had to take them. We were tested orally if we were deemed to be too ill to write. I much preferred oral exams and quite enjoyed that experience – as a general rule I hated exams.

Food was becoming more of a problem and I remember my mother being puzzled at the constant requests for Pan Yan pickle. We used this to put on our greens, particularly the sprouts, which came to the table full of little black beetles and the pickle was used to cover them up and make them easier to eat. We were always hungry and ate piles of bread. In the early days we had jam from home, but it didn't last long so we would write off for sample pots of Marmite. They were only half-ounce pots but were better than nothing. If anyone was sent something special from home it was definitely *de rigueur* to share it with your friends. I remember a bar of Aero chocolate disappearing at the speed of light amongst my sudden host of 'friends', and being left with one piece.

I returned to London to live at home sometime in 1941, the rest of the school returning a term or two later. I had become completely disillusioned with boarding school and my parents felt the worst of the London bombing was over. It was such a relief to be home. We had a Morrison shelter in the dining room, which I slept in every night and my parents would join me if there was an air-raid. My father was in the Home Guard, my mother was doing war work in a local telecommunications factory and I cycled to school every day. Life seemed infinitely better all of a sudden. I joined the Girl Guides and made a lot of new friends out of school. I spent summer holidays out of London for weeks at a time, first with my mother in Norfolk at her brother's farm and then in Skegness with friends of friends. We went to the cinema frequently, often queuing for hours to see a popular film, and the local swimming pool was a meeting place for 'our gang' even if it meant cycling four miles there and back. The joy was the absolutely wonderful chocolate cake that they were still producing in the café.

I had almost two summers off school during the war, firstly with a double mastoid and then with my appendicitis. I was one of the first patients to be given the new wonder drug M & B, and it dispersed my mastoid and saved me from having an operation. I was very relieved. My mother, who had never been really ill in her life, decided that the walk home from the hospital – about four miles, it was near the swimming pool – was perfectly within my capabilities. She was shocked, and afterwards very remorseful, when she realised, as I weakly asked if we could sit down as we were going through the park about half-way home, that I was not totally up to speed.

Life at school was kept as normal as possible. I remember taking my scholarship exams in the cellar or basement amongst piles of wood and other stored items and feeling quite excited at the strangeness of my surroundings. The nuns were obviously determined that we should be as unaffected by the war as possible and there was certainly no let-up in the rigour of our education. When 'doodle-bugs', as the V1 flying bombs were commonly known, started falling on London I can remember listening for the engine noise to stop and then running into a shop doorway on my way home from Guides one Friday night. We were taken on our first Guide camp during this time and, unfortunately, a doodle-bug had fallen in the garden of one of our number the night before we were to set off. No doubt her parents thought that going off to camp in the country would be a good way of keeping her safe but delayed shock set in during the first night we were away and we all had to come home the next day.

VE night remains vividly in my memory. My father, who was not given to public demonstrations of joy, surprised me by taking me to every neighbouring street to enjoy the partying that was in full swing. He also took my mother and me up into the centre of London (and he hated crowds!), and we joined the masses of people outside Buckingham Palace and in St James's Park. It was a wonderful experience.

Three Little Maids from School
Marguerite (Jill) Day née Cady: Christine (Tommy) Gilbert née Cross: Beryl Stringer née Sharman

Three schoolgirls who attended the Walberswick Primary School at the outbreak of war became great friends and have remained so over the years.

SCHOOL CHILDREN

They meet every year to have a meal and talk over old times and bring each other up to date on what they have been doing over the past year. The girls are Jill Day née Cady, Christine ('Tommy') Gilbert née Cross, and Beryl Stringer née Sharman. They all now live in different parts of Suffolk. This story is theirs and tells of how they, as Walberswick school children, saw the war and how it affected them. Because each story is told separately there will be a repetition of some tales but described in a different way as the personalities of each of them show through.

Jill's story

I was seven years old when war was declared and really didn't know what it meant for the country to be at war. It soon became rather exciting, though, when we were issued with gas masks and identity cards and saw the village filling up with soldiers.

We were given gas mask drill and practised using a stirrup pump, which was a portable hand-operated pump with a footrest and used with a bucket of water to extinguish small fires. I also remember having sleeps in the afternoon at school due to lack of sleep at night when the German planes were overhead and we were disturbed by exploding bombs and the noise of anti-aircraft guns firing.

The village filling up with troops with their lorries, jeeps, and other vehicles was really thrilling and watching them drill and marching to church on

Jill as a bride with her groom Arthur Day.
(Photo from Jill Day)

JILL'S STORY

Sundays was fascinating. When the Cameronians arrived they really caught our imagination with the band wearing their kilts and practising and playing the bagpipes on the village green. The troops were very friendly and taught us Highland dancing and in the winter they would join in the fun helping us to build snowmen and having snowball fights. Summer-time saw us fishing in the creek from the Sluice Bridge with a little help from these new-found friends.

The Barn Cinema, owned by Ronald Jeans, provided us with many an enthralling evening. We also had what was known as the Shack Club which was run by the Revd Dix, the soldiers' chaplain, and his wife and through Mr and Mrs Jeans we were encouraged to organise and perform entertainments of our own in order to raise funds for the Red Cross. Mrs Dix introduced us to the writings of Paul Gallico and I especially remember her reading to us his book, *The Snow Goose*. These were happy times when all the village children were involved in these activities. Even though we were short of sweets and fruit we remained in good spirits and exciting things were always happening.

I remember one particular occasion when tea chests were washed up on the beach; they were collected and we scooped tea into bags from the opened chests and took them home. At that time very little of the beach was open to us; most of it had scaffolding at the water's edge with iron spikes buried on the seaward side and it was also heavily mined. We swam a lot from the mine-free stretch of beach during the summer and would also play down by the river. I have a permanent reminder of those times when I caught my leg on one of the spikes and had to go to Southwold hospital and have it stitched.

There was one time I remember when I saw a stretcher was being carried along the street to Fisher's Garage and saw two large boots sticking out of the end. It really didn't register that it was a corpse. I was just told a body had been washed up on the beach.

I do remember being frightened once when I was at Walberswick School and there was an air-raid alert. We were not allowed to leave school during air-raid alerts, but this time the alert seemed to go on for ages and as there was no sign of any activity, Mrs Piper, our schoolmistress, told us we could leave in twos to go home. So Richard Buggs, who lived not too far from me, and I were told we could go. We had just neared the end of the school building and were about to cross

SCHOOL CHILDREN

the playground when I heard this awful noise and, pulling Richard with me, rushed back into the school. We were just in time – the noise had been a German bomber flying very low, machine-gunning and dropping bombs on Southwold. I found out later that Mr Palmer, the ferryman was rowing my aunt, Maud Cady, across the river at the time. Luckily neither bullets nor bombs hit them.

We had evacuees in the village and this caused riots with the village children. I remember they were very unruly in school and were always getting the cane from the schoolmistress.

When I was 10 years old I went to Reydon Area Council School by bus. There were lots of air raids going on at this time and we would have to go in file to the shelters situated on the school playing field. We were frequently late getting home from school because the bus was not allowed to leave if there was an air raid going on.

We often collected shrapnel to take to school after an air raid. At times the village organised a 'War Effort Week' and we children would collect salvage from around the village consisting of tins, paper, bottles, and other recyclable items. These would be taken to the farm stack yard and stored for pick-up later by the authorities.

Mrs Shepherd, who was the area organiser of the Land Girls, ran a Rabbit Club. Practically everyone in the village kept rabbits to supplement the meagre meat ration. During harvest time we would spend lots of time in the harvest field hoping to catch a rabbit; we would also go blackberry picking and the fruit was given to the W.I. to make jam. We children were also encouraged to knit scarves and gloves to be sent to the armed forces.

I vividly remember the first doodlebug (V1) I heard; it sounded like a very noisy motorbike – they were scary. Later, we would quite regularly, when waiting for the school bus at the Anchor Inn, see vapour trails on the horizon out at sea. We were told these were from the V2 rockets being launched from Holland and aimed at London.

When the troops moved out of the village and before the new ones arrived we used to scrump the fruit from the gardens of the houses they had occupied. The Nissen huts the soldiers lived in were often decorated with murals and pin-ups of Jane of the *Daily Mirror* and other girls of the same type.

We occasionally helped peel potatoes and other vegetables at the cookhouse and the soldiers would sometimes reward us with tins of sweets, which they would buy from the NAAFI – this was a great treat for us.

When an aircraft crashed, as they often did in this area we would cycle to the spot, but of course were not allowed to go too close. We watched bombers, hundreds of them, flying out and then, some hours later, see them coming back, in ones and twos, many of them really crippled with silent engines and damage to the fuselage and wings. I didn't realise the significance of all this until much later after the war had ended.

I remember the hush over the village prior to D-Day when suddenly all the troops had gone. It seemed so strange and odd. Of course at the time we didn't know why or where they had all gone to.

There were celebrations when the war was over but I cannot remember what they were, I only know that life for me as a 13 year old schoolgirl was never as exciting again.

Tommy's story

I remember before the war actually started adults talking about it – some saying it wouldn't come to anything and others excited by the prospect.

I was eight years old when the war began. Mostly all my family lived in the village. My maternal grandparents, Mr and Mrs Horace Fairs, farmed the Manor Farm and Eastwood Lodge on the outskirts of the village. My mother and father and older sister Daphne lived at Dunwich View at the top of the village green, part of which was the Manor Farm Dairy Shop. The BBC Home Service news told us war had been declared against Germany. The 'Jerrys' had already reported for duty and the call-up of our troops were starting.

We were given identity cards with a number, which we were told to memorise. Gas masks came, we were shown how to put them on at school and carried them at all times in a cardboard box with a string strap. Later when the boxes became dog-eared some of us had more up-market cases of canvas or Rexine.

SCHOOL CHILDREN

The school windows were covered in a sticky net material to protect us from flying glass. Most windows of houses were criss-crossed with sticky tape. An ARP Warden instructed us how to put out an incendiary bomb fire with a stirrup pump and a bucket of water. All torches had a half-moon cardboard put over the top half to stop light going upward being seen by enemy aircraft. Blackout curtains or blankets were drawn at night before turning on electric lights – the patrolling ARP Warden would be sure to see if we let any light escape.

Miss Parker from Dickon Nurseries was a St John's Ambulance officer and we were shown by her how to roll bandages, put slings on broken arms, and how to apply pressure on pressure points to stop bleeding.

Tommy sitting on Walberswick Common.
(Photo from Christine Gilbert)

TOMMY'S STORY

We had tests and were given certificates and a badge to show we belonged to the St John's.

Salvage collections were started – the iron railings from the front of Dunwich View were taken to melt down for bombs. Some families had Anderson shelters dug in their gardens but we had a steel Morrison table shelter with mesh around the sides. I can truthfully say that the only times I can remember being really scared was having to sleep in that thing, dreading to be buried alive. Nearly all other war memories are mostly exciting – some sadness of course, especially about Uncle Jim Cross missing at Singapore, prisoner of the Japs. Granny Cross hoping her boy was all right. What a blessing she didn't know at the time of the deprivation, starvation, and cruelty the prisoners were receiving at the hands of the Nips. [See *Suffolk Memories,* pp. 1–5, for more about Lance Cpl James Cross, 4th Battalion. Suffolk Regiment.]

At school we were warned not to pick up any interesting objects we found lying on the ground. The Germans were dropping nice things to tempt children to pick them up, which would then explode and if not kill us would probably blow off our fingers. I once found a fountain pen lying in the grass on the village green and after a while I gave in to temptation and picked it up half expecting an explosion. I remember feeling a bit peeved when, after having risked all to pick the thing up, I then had to hand it over for it to be claimed.

Sometimes at night we would watch the searchlights criss-crossing the sky, occasionally picking up a plane, the guns firing, and later picking up pieces of shrapnel as souvenirs. For years after the war we kept polished brass bullet cases standing on our mantelshelf.

The moneyed families left the village for safer areas and their houses were then requisitioned either for the evacuees who came from the East End of London or for the army, the village being full of soldiers.

Village life was not to the liking of most of the evacuees but the pubs did very well from them. I had a feeling, though, that Mrs Piper, the village schoolteacher, and many of the village inhabitants were somewhat relieved when they moved on, or went back to London to take their chances in the Blitz.

We were expecting an invasion: the Germans were at the ready the other side of the water. I sometimes watched from the top windows of our house out to sea, half expecting to see them coming. We kept a bag

SCHOOL CHILDREN

packed ready, because in the event of an invasion we would be taken further inland, to Halesworth I think.

My father Harold Cross (people called him 'Sonny') was a Coastguard, and he with Mr Harold Piper, Mr Henry Block and Mr Herbert (known locally as 'Scarborough') English had a lookout hut on the beach, which had to be manned 24 hours a day. They only had two rifles between the four of them. The beach had been mined, scaffolding erected along the waterline with concrete anti-tank blocks in rows along the back of the beach. They would patrol the beach, meet with the Coastguards coming from Dunwich, and report and help to recover bodies and other items washed up on the beach. Sometimes they would get machine-gunned by passing German planes. I well remember watching from the corner seat the men carrying a body on a board to, I think, a shed at the back of the Anchor Hotel. They carried the body with respect, covered, or nearly covered for his feet were sticking out at the bottom, with the board resting on their shoulders as if it were a coffin.

One night a bomb exploded behind our house knocking down part of the Old Vicarage. My father who was on watch on the beach at the time saw, by the light of the explosions, tiles flying off our house and he thought our house had been hit. We were inside the house and were enveloped in a cloud of floating 'something'. I thought it was gas but it was only soot from the chimneys and plaster from the ceiling.

This brings to mind the time when a Mrs Taylor's house in Short Lane was bombed. She was inside at the time but came out of the wreckage fairly unscathed.

To those unfamiliar with Walberswick: before the war a steam-powered ferry ran between Walberswick and Southwold, hauled back and forth by a heavy chain.

The ferry was unchained and left for some time lying on the side of the river and all signposts were removed.

I remember the sentries in a concrete pillbox by the Tower House challenging all entering the village after dark: 'Halt. Who goes there, friend or foe?'; answer: 'Friend'; reply: 'Advance friend and be recognised.' Whereupon you walked forward showed your identity card, had a chat with the sentry, and walked on.

TOMMY'S STORY

We knitted scarves, fingerless mitts etc. for the forces, but I can't remember being very good at that. I think the sum total of my efforts might have been one scarf. At school we did knit poke bonnets in various shades of itchy wool.

Clothing coupons were issued but they did not run to much more than shoes. As we outgrew our coats and dresses they were lengthened with wide bands of different materials around the hems. Something shop-bought was exciting, even if it was only from Mrs Reynolds drapers shop.

To supplement the meat ration Mrs Shepherd ran a rabbit club for the children and we had rabbits, supposedly to produce offspring. I shared a rabbit with a boy called Henry Lee and we kept it at a Miss Fincham's down the Lea. The does were mated with the buck, which was kept at Mrs Shepherd's. We were not allowed to see the mating bit.

After our doe had her litter Henry would keep poking the nest to count how many baby rabbits she had. The doe would bring them out dead, having killed them herself because they had been looked at by Henry. She would leave the bodies in a row by the hutch door. So our contribution didn't help out the meat ration. Every so often meat pies were sold from the Women's Institute hut.

I remember with great affection Mrs Catchpole and Mrs Meekins who ran the Chapel Sunday school. They always gave us a nice time with parties, etc. We had community hymn singing once a week and many soldiers joined in, some singing solos. It was all good loud stuff with Mrs Meekins playing the organ.

For entertainment there was the Barn Cinema, owned by Mr Ronald Jeans. It had a well-equipped projection room and my sister Daphne sometimes ran it. We booked our nine-penny [3¾p] seats. The stage had Hollywood-type curtains and on the walls were signed photographs of film stars. We knew all the names of the Hollywood film stars, especially after the Yanks came. On occasions we village kids took part in a live show. We did a lot of singing and learned all the words of the wartime songs from sheet music. Mock auctions were held in the Gannon Room; articles were donated, then put up for auction. The highest bidder gave the money but it was returned as savings stamps for War Loan [Bonds].

SCHOOL CHILDREN

Because I was long and thin they said I was like a 'pull-through' (something to clean the rifle barrel with). My sister was six years my senior and pretty and was invited to dances and dinners at the U.S. base at Holton where they had masses of ice cream. We didn't get a lot of that. Older sisters had all the fun; we were always too young. Daphne was in the Land Army and worked at my grandfather's farm with two other girls, Joyce Hambling and Dulcie Goodwin. They milked the herd of red polls and did all kinds of farm work including driving the horse and cart. There was only one tractor and I don't believe they were allowed to drive that. Sometimes German prisoners were brought to work on the land and they would boil potatoes in the wash copper to eat with their meals. I believe they wore grey overalls. I never spoke to them, they were the enemy, but I do remember they looked very serious, down-in-the-mouth type people and I was told that nobody tried to escape.

As a hobby we collected cigarette cards from the soldiers and swapped them to get sets. I don't remember much about the rationing. The sweet coupons were about 2 oz or maybe 4 oz a week. Choosing what to have took time; chocolate-covered Blue Bird toffees were a favourite and maybe sherbet. I remember being told once of chocolate in tiny little squares that was called 'Exlax' that was not rationed. It turned out to be a patent medicine used if you were constipated; I never had any but I knew somebody who did.

Certain people with foreign connections were being interned and we children were sure one or two were still in the village, one person especially we were sure was a spy. We followed her a lot hoping to catch her giving signals to German ships at sea. I can't remember what happened but I guess we gave up in the end.

We listened to the news on the radio but most of the best stuff was from overheard adult conversations – brave deeds – narrow escapes – and a few reputations going down the drain. We did sometimes follow round the lane soldiers walking out with their girl friends until we were glared at and told to clear off.

We would sit on the green to watch the troops at their drill, being shouted at by the sergeants and sergeant majors. One sergeant major I remember well would make men drill over and over again. One day a man in full pack fainted and fell – other soldiers picked him up and put him by a garden wall. The weather was very cold and snowing; we wondered if he would be punished for not doing the drill – maybe even shot.

The soldiers would play snowballs with us and at one time we had big snowmen on the green. Later we saw the sergeant major marching, or walking smartly into the gateway of a village house which was being used as the Officer's Mess. We threw snowballs at him and one knocked his hat or cap off, I remember well him whipping round and glaring at us. We didn't throw any more but we really thought that in our way we had paid him back for being so nasty to the man who fainted and we had probably taught him a lesson.

When the Cameronians arrived, the pipe band, which was stationed in the Terrace, would practise playing their pipes, banging their drums and marching up and down the village green. (My father would sometimes be trying to get a bit of sleep if he had been on Coastguard watch all night, so was not too keen.) We children loved them; they paraded about in kilts, and did highland dancing and the sword dance and taught us the Highland Fling. They came to the village whist

*The Cameronians in their trews in Walberswick School playground.
(Photo from Christine Gilbert)*

SCHOOL CHILDREN

drives, played darts and were very well liked by all the village people. Then gradually the soldiers left the village leaving a few behind as rear guards. Something big was going on, so everybody said.

I clearly remember watching as wave after wave of bombers passed over, heading outward from the airfields. There were more planes than I had ever seen before. By this time in the war we were well accustomed to watching the German doodle bugs chugging along, being shot at from the shore-gun batteries and seeing our planes limping back after bombing raids with bits missing and engines on the blink. But this was different, D-Day had arrived – now we were winning at last.

My father had a big map on the wall, and as the news came through on the radio he would stick little pins on name places. 'Monty' seemed the most talked of General. He'd already won desert victories with Desert Rats and the war was being won in Europe. But then came the news and 'Pathé' pictures of the death camps were shown. That was really nightmare stuff and I think for the first time I realised that our experience of the war was so different. We'd been so lucky. Hitler was dead, the war was over, VE Day celebrations began. But it was not all good. We were sad for the families who had lost their loved ones and we were five years older now, and in our teens. Our war had been a bit scary at times, we were rationed but never hungry, and most of the time it was all quite exciting. As village children we had experiences of meeting and making friends from all over the British Isles, American Yanks, white and black. The whites could not understand why we British did not have a colour bar. The war had not been like that for others; we then started seeing films of the terrible things that had happened in Russia, the German death camps, atomic bombs on Japan and other ghastly happenings. I was very glad to have spent my war being an ordinary Walberswick village kid.

Beryl's story

I was nine years old when war broke out and my memories of the war years are much the same as Jill's and Tommy's. I remember standing around the army cookhouse and talking to the soldiers. Also the army concerts in the Gannon Room and going to see films in the Barn Cinema and sometimes a concert. Although it was exciting seeing all

BERYL'S STORY

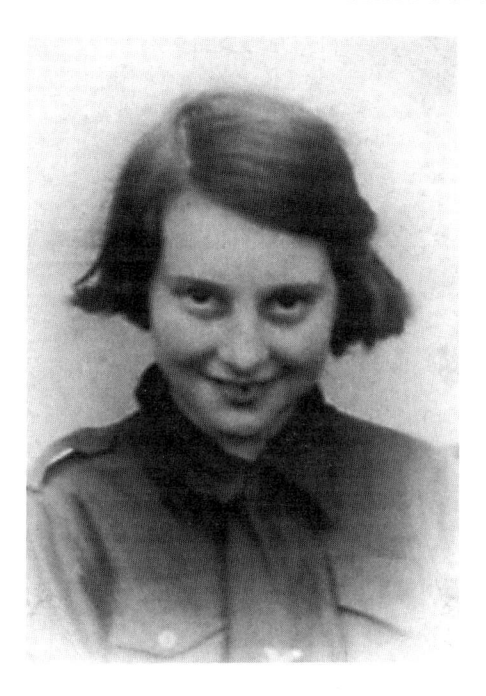

the soldiers coming into the village, when the Camer- onians arrived they really caught the imagination, wearing their kilts and marching up and down the village green playing the bagpipes.

On a more serious note I remember whenever the air raid siren went off listening for the sound of the German planes; they had a very different sound to ours. Also I remember the times when my mother and I would stand watching out of our upstairs back bedroom window looking at the V1 flying bombs coming in over the sea. We would pray that the light from the engine wouldn't go out because if it did that meant it had reached its target and would shortly dive to the ground and explode. I will never forget the feeling of great relief when the 'All Clear' siren sounded after an air raid.

Beryl Sharman in her Brownies' uniform after being evacuated to Buckinghamshire. (Photo from Beryl Stringer)

We had a Morrison shelter in our kitchen, which was like a big iron table where we went under when there was an air raid.

When we went to school we always had to carry our gas masks and I recall that after a night raid we would be given a sleeping time period.

When my eldest brother who was in the army came on leave, my friends and I loved to stand round the piano for a sing-song while he played all the tunes of those times. It was an awful time for us when the telegram came through to my mum and dad telling them that he had been wounded; and this really brought home to me what a frightening thing war was.

SCHOOL CHILDREN

In our house we always had to be quiet when the news came on from the Home Service of the BBC. We would also listen to Lord Haw-Haw, the propaganda broadcaster from Germany, but we didn't take much notice of him especially after he had broadcast that the important railway junction of Southwold had been bombed. [Lord Haw-Haw's real name was William Joyce, a British citizen; after the war he was hanged as a traitor.]

When there was a rumour of an invasion my mum and dad sent me to Buckinghamshire where my eldest sister was nursing; it was certainly much quieter there, air-raid-wise. I was there less than a year, as I became quite homesick. At one time my parents and Jill's guardian, her aunt Maud, talked about sending us to Australia for the duration of the war, but when news came that a ship carrying children had been torpedoed that put an end to that plan. [This was probably the *City of Benares* torpedoed on 17 September 1940, on its way to Canada when 77 evacuee children were drowned.]

I also remember seeing the huge crater made by a land mine in the tennis court of the Old Vicarage down by the ferry and heard the terrific explosion of two American aircraft that had collided in mid-air and crashed not far from Eastwood Lodge Farm. My sister Eileen, who was a nurse at Blythburgh hospital, was engaged to an American airman, Don Holbert, stationed at Holton and she was off duty and at home that day. When she heard the explosion she had a premonition that Don's plane, Paper Doll, was one of the aircraft that had crashed. I remember it was a Wednesday and half-day closing so I, with Eileen and my friend Jill, cycled up to the scene to look for anything that would identify the plane or any of the airmen who had been killed. The first thing we found to our horror was a foot with its sock still on. Eileen went over to it and turned back the sock to see if there happened to be any name on it but there was nothing. Suddenly she spotted a piece of the fuselage and painted on it was the name Paper Doll, Don's plane. It was a dreadful shock to all three of us but especially, of course, to Eileen and it broke her heart.

Shortly after Don was killed Eileen penned the following:[1]

---

[1] This poem is very personal to its author who requests that no copies be made of it: to do so will infringe the copyright © of this book.

BERYL'S STORY

LEST WE FORGET

The peace bells have rung out; the world is now at rest,
But many hearts are aching for they have lost their best.
The wives and sweethearts thinking of their own lost loved ones;
The mothers' hearts are aching too for their lost brave sons.
We never can repay the debts although we have Victory,
For each brave boy and man who died to help set us free.
Then there are all the wounded, the shocked, the blind, the lame;
Every one joined in to help bring back peace again.
They all joined in to help, the men and women too,
Not everybody wore a dress of khaki or of blue.
Old men became the Home Guard and some a factory hand;
While some young girls were nurses and others on the land.
Now they have got their full reward, they did not work in vain,
For some have got their loved ones back with them again.
Although they may be wounded shocked or lost a limb
Each loving heart looks proud and thinks, 'well I still have got him'.
But then, what of the lonely; the ones who lost their all?
Their loved ones had to answer that heavenly trumpet call.
So let us not forget them when we pray to God above
And ask that they may meet again the ones they lost but love.

Composed by Eileen Amara Sharman 19 October 1944
In loving memory of D.V.H.

Beryl's story continues:

The last year of the war I worked at Mr Reynolds's grocer shop in Walberswick and clearly remember weighing up the weekly ration per person. I believe it was 2oz of butter, 2oz of lard, 4oz of margarine, ½lb sugar, 3oz of cheese (agricultural workers were allowed more cheese but I cannot bring to mind the amount). There was a monthly ration of 1lb of jam and ½lb of tea per person. The ration books were three different colours: green for very young children (up to five years I think), blue for the older children, and buff for adults. Certain foods could only be got on a green or blue book. There was also a points system and you had 24 points a month: canned foods were so many points per tin and I remember Golden Syrup, when you could get it which was not very often, being 8 points for a 1lb tin. Everything was in short supply, but Mr Reynolds worked out a very fair system – he always waited until he had enough of a particular item making it available for everybody for one week and this gave everybody an equal chance to have their share. Also I remember having to make up bags from newspaper to weigh the soap flakes which came in a sack; not a very nice job as the dust used to get up one's nose and make you sneeze.

I used to sleep in the attic and when peace was declared I remember an aeroplane coming overhead and thanking God how wonderful it was to know that never again need I fear the noise of a plane coming overhead.